J. M. SYNGE AND THE WESTERN MIND

J. M. SYNGE
AND THE WESTERN MIND

Weldon Thornton

Irish Literary Studies 4

COLIN SMYTHE
Gerrards Cross, Bucks
1979

Copyright © 1979 Colin Smythe Ltd.

First published in 1979 by Colin Smythe Ltd.,
Gerrards Cross, Buckinghamshire

British Library Cataloguing in Publication Data

Thornton, Weldon
J. M. Synge and the Western mind – (Irish literary
studies; 4; 0140-895X).
1. Synge, John Millington – Criticism and interpretation
I. Title   II. Series
822′.9′12   PR5534

ISBN 0-901072-89-3

Printed in Great Britain
Set by Watford Typesetters Ltd., and printed and bound by
Billing & Sons Ltd., Guildford, Worcester and London

For
David, Clayton, Stephen

Contents

Acknowledgments

In my several years of work toward this book, I have received help from many institutions and persons. A grant from the American Council of Learned Societies enabled me to spend the summer of 1973 in Dublin. A grant from the University of North Carolina Research Council gave me the Fall Semester of 1973 free from teaching duties, so that I could put my ideas into coherent form. These ideas were earlier tried out on students in several of my classes, and I owe them thanks for their confirmations and their challenges. My colleague Joseph M. Flora also deserves thanks for his reading and criticism of the manuscript. The staff of the Louis Round Wilson Library of the University of North Carolina has helped me in ways too various to acknowledge.

I am grateful to the Oxford University Press for permission to quote from Synge's *Collected Works*, and to the Synge Estate for permission to quote from unpublished manuscript material.

While in Dublin I drew repeatedly upon the knowledge and good will of the staff of the Rare Book Room in Trinity College, and especially of Miss Mary Pollard. My thanks are due to Dr William O'Sullivan, Keeper of Manuscripts in Trinity College, for making available the extensive collection of Synge material, and to all of the Manuscripts Room staff for their generous help. Finally, my special thanks go to Mrs Lilo Stephens for permission to use the Typescript Biography of Synge by her late husband, Edward M. Stephens, and to Dr. Andrew Carpenter of University College, Dublin, for his many kinds of help.

Introduction

Several years ago I realized that the implicit sense of the personality of J. M. Synge I received from reading his writings did not match up with the impressions gained from reading accounts of him. Most of those accounts, whether by those who knew him such as W. B. Yeats or John Masefield, or by scholars such as Maurice Bourgeois or David H. Greene, depicted a man of considerable intellectual self-confidence, and one indifferent to issues of politics or religion. Linked with this was the claim that Synge was largely alienated from his religiously and socially orthodox family, and that he owed little to them. The point about Synge's indifference to religion especially evoked my scepticism, even though this opinion seemed almost universal among those who knew him and it forms an important part of the interpretation presented in the biography by David H. Greene and Edward M. Stephens.[1] The more closely I read Synge's works, the less satisfactory the view of Synge as aloof and indifferent seemed to me. I became convinced that there were eddies beneath the surface that had gone largely unnoticed or unappreciated. I suspected that Synge's mother was a strong influence on his life, though it was clear he could not accept her religious doctrines. I came also to doubt whether Synge possessed the olympian self-confidence and independence Yeats had attributed to him. But most of all, I came to feel that Synge had been strongly marked by his family's religious milieu and that while he may have reacted against that or may have redefined its contents, he remained a man of deeply religious temperament, a man to whom religious and political beliefs were of great importance.

As I continued to pursue these ideas, I realized my dissatisfaction with another facet of the interpretation of Synge's career. I had to agree that Yeats and others were right in seeing Synge's experiences on the Aran Islands as being fundamental to the emergence of his genius. Undoubtedly Synge's sojourns on those islands did contribute immensely to his almost magical transforma-

11

tion from an unconfident amateur who hid his literary aspirations behind a facade of philological interest, into a skillful dramatist. But the explanations that were given for this transformation seemed insufficient, even superficial. General opinion was that Synge had found on the islands various folk stories and plots and a living language, and that these enabled him to become a writer; but I felt that the change was more fundamental than plots and language could account for.

In the summer of 1973, an ACLS grant enabled me to go to Dublin to examine unpublished documents by and about Synge. Reading Synge's Notebooks in the collection of Trinity College was indeed helpful to me, but even more important was my reading of the Typescript biography of Synge written by his nephew, Edward M. Stephens.[2] Since I knew that this Typescript had formed part of the foundation of the Greene/Stephens biography, I had not expected it to contain much new to me. To my surprise and pleasure, I found that the Typescript was in some ways significantly different from the published biography. Most important for me, it gave a different impression of Synge's religious sensibilities and a fuller picture of his relationships with his family. Stephens shows that Synge was unable to accept his family's doctrines, but was nevertheless influenced by their religious milieu and by the personality of his mother. Stephens's account stresses Synge's high regard for the truth and for the integrity of his own mind, and his consequent inability to dissemble about his lack of belief.

As I reread Synge's published and unpublished works in the light of insights gained and suspicions confirmed by the Stephens Typescript, I began to see a strand running through his personality and his works. I began to see that for Synge ideas, beliefs, were not trivial; they were on the contrary of such importance that the theme of the power of ideas, especially of implicit ideas, runs throughout his life and work. The strand begins with Synge's learning from his family to value truth and the integrity of beliefs; it is first clearly manifested in the shock he felt when his reading Darwin threw everything he had known about natural science and religion into a new perspective. After this shock, he turned to works of 'Christian evidence' and to rationalism in an attempt to solve his dilemma or assuage his guilt over his apostasy, but he could not reconcile his own beliefs with those of his family, nor could he reconcile the importance he was drawn into giving to ideas with his own sense of the importance of the affective dimension of experience. He was, then, victimized by the content and the authority of the ideas in his milieu.

Seeing Synge's early development as involving an intellectual crisis enabled me better to understand why his sojourns on the Aran Islands were so fruitful for him. For there Synge found not simply plots and language, but something more fundamental to his development. There he found a world view so different from the one he had been reared in that it was like breathing a new atmosphere. He found enticements to ideas and attitudes that had until now been latent in him. More important, he saw how different were the implicit beliefs of these islanders from those he had imbibed, and through this he began to realize how variable and arbitrary a role received ideas play in our experience. He had truly come into a new world, one characterized both by different ideas than his own, and by a strikingly different attitude toward the authority of ideas. While Synge had agonized over his inability to accept his family's beliefs, here he found a people who without guilt blended Catholic orthodoxy and paganism. They moved with apparent ease between what should have been incompatible modes of thought.

As I reread Synge's plays with these issues in mind, I saw that his dramatic canon was, among other things, a consistent, even progressive exploration of concerns or insights growing out of his youthful struggles with his family's religious and social milieu, and his revelatory experiences on the Aran Islands. Every play in some way reflects Synge's concern with the power of ideas. In some instances this expresses itself in Synge's wish to shock his audience by evoking and then challenging or undermining some aesthetic stereotype or some political or religious doctrine. In others it occurs in his wish to do dramatic justice to a cultural milieu so alien to that of his audience that they can hardly conceive it. Often it occurs as a dramatic confrontation between individuals who express qualitatively different life styles or cultures. The theme may occur as a deeper exploration, pessimistic or optimistic, of the philosophical implications of asking what relation there is between idea and 'reality'. It may even occur as Synge's own attempt to elude his contemporaries' stereotyped attitudes toward traditional dramatic material. But throughout we see Synge wrestling with these issues.

This book is, then, an attempt to show the importance both to Synge's mind and to his art of a coherent set of themes. It is neither a full scale intellectual biography, nor does it provide new interpretations of each of the plays. Rather, it follows one recurrent strand through the mind and the work. In the first chapter, the emphasis is upon showing how Synge's familial milieu contributed to his development and on illustrating the importance to him of religious issues and of 'opinions' generally. The second chapter is a necessary complement to the first, in that we cannot understand what happened to Synge on the Aran Islands without knowing something of the quality of that world; Chapter II argues that the world Synge found was one that deserves to be called archaic, one characterized both by different received ideas than Synge had known and by a different attitude toward the authority of abstractions. Chapter III turns to *The Aran Islands*, the book that most fully reflects the coming together of the man and the milieu and that shows us what aspects of the islands most attracted and influenced Synge. Chapters IV, V, and VI discuss the effects of Synge's experiences and insights in his plays. Variable as these effects are, there is a progression in Synge's exploration, and the chapter divisions reflect this. Chapter III discusses specific expressions of these themes in Synge's first three plays. Chapter V pairs Synge's first two full length plays, because, while they re-employ some devices from earlier plays, they are best seen as complementary dramatizations of philosophical issues beneath the themes we are tracing. The last chapter deals with Synge's final play, *Deirdre of the Sorrows*, since it is a new departure for Synge, an application of what he had learned from exploring these themes through the first five plays.

NOTES

1. David H. Greene and Edward M. Stephens, *J. M. Synge, 1871-1909* (New York, 1959), is the standard biography. As Greene explains in the 'Introduction,' the biography is a joint product of himself and Synge's nephew, Edward M. Stephens. Stephens worked for years on what he hoped would be a biography of his uncle, but the typescript grew to such length – nearly three quarters of a million words, according to Greene – that it proved unwieldly and was rejected by several publishers. In 1953 Stephens asked Greene whether he would collaborate on the project. Early in 1955 Stephens died, and his wife, Mrs Lilo Stephens, then suggested that Greene write a biography using her husband's material and naming him as joint author. The result was, as Greene says, 'a book quite different from the one Edward Stephens projected' (p. ix). I shall refer to this work as the Greene/Stephens biography.
2. This Typescript is one of my main biographical sources; I shall cite it parenthetically as TS. Since few of the passages I quote are included in Andrew Carpenter's *My Uncle John* (Oxford, 1975), and since the Typescript is now available as part of the Trinity College collection, my citations are to the Typescript, not to Carpenter's edition.

I

Seed Time of the Soul

i

The purpose of this biographical chapter is not to provide an account of the life of J. M. Synge; that is available in the Greene/Stephens biography.[1] My aim here is to highlight aspects of Synge's temperament, his development, and his familial relationships, that are relevant to the ideas within this study, emphasizing those factors that prepared Synge to appreciate and respond to what he found on the Aran Islands. Before turning to these, some problems facing anyone attempting to delve into Synge's personality should be acknowledged. In a lecture at the Synge Centenary celebration in Dublin in 1971, David H. Greene made what he called an 'unusual admission' for a biographer – he said that Synge's 'personality has always struck me as being unchangingly enigmatic.'[2] Anyone who has tried to pursue Synge's track will understand Greene's admission. Synge was indeed a taciturn man, a man who revealed himself to very few. In his lecture, Greene spoke of 'the only two men who knew Synge well' (p. 180), naming Stephen MacKenna and John Masefield. While I am sceptical about how well Masefield knew Synge,[3] I accept Greene's underlying point that Synge was reserved, that few people saw beneath the surface, and that to most of those who knew him, he remained a mystery. We must, then, be cautious in accepting contemporary descriptions of Synge as more than suggestions for consideration. But if his reserve is on the one hand a barrier to our seeing into the man, it is on the other an important part of the 'evidence' about him. It is one of the most important traits of his character, remarked by almost all who met him, and an interpretation of Synge's personality should explore its sources and its meaning.

A related problem is the ubiquity and authority of W. B. Yeats's comments about Synge. Though Yeats and Synge were closely associated for many years, and each influenced the other, I cannot

15

include Yeats among those who knew Synge well (nor does Greene). Yeats's understanding of Synge was sporadic and was influenced by his own theories of personality and his own needs. Some of Yeats's comments about Synge, especially about his art, show great insight; others, about his self-confidence or his indifference to theories and beliefs, reflect a superficial view of Synge and tell us more about what Yeats wished Synge to be than what he was. Yet Yeats's statements have strongly colored the portrait of Synge we have inherited. Early commentators especially, faced with a dearth of information, relied upon the statements of this man whom they presumed knew Synge well. But Yeats's statements about Synge, though occasionally penetrating, are unreliable and must be used tentatively.[4]

ii

No one questions that Synge's familial situation had a strong, even a determining, influence on his character and on his attitudes toward life and art. But discussions of Synge's relationship with his family have dwelt upon his inability to accept their orthodoxy and their inability to understand his artistic aspirations. According to this view, Synge was an outsider, an alien from the family. No doubt Synge did find it impossible to accept his family's orthodoxy, and they in turn were largely obtuse about his aspirations. But emphasis on his alienation obscures the fact that Synge remained a part of his family throughout his life, and that they provided his primary, almost his sole, social context. More important, it clouds the significant influence their religious attitudes had on his own view of life and of art. This is especially true of his mother, who, for all the limitations of her sensibility, was one of the greatest influences, positive and negative, on Synge. But while he suffered considerable guilt about his inability to accept his family's beliefs, and while their insistence upon doctrinal agreement was alien to his temperament, their religious attitudes did strongly influence his own world view.

The received view of Synge's personality dwells also upon his supposed insensitivity to, even indifference toward, religious issues, and upon his being a rationalist. But he was not indifferent to religious questions, and his rationalism was superficial. It would be truer to say that he remained too acutely concerned about matters of belief, or that the issue of belief – especially the congruence between opinion and feeling, between abstraction and emotion – was of crucial importance to him.

Synge was, as David H. Greene explains, reared in a household permeated by orthodoxy – religious, social, political, and economic. The Synge family was of the evangelical strand of the Church of Ireland, was of the land-owning class, and was unionist and royalist in politics. Of the five surviving children, Samuel became a medical missionary to China, Robert became a prosperous owner of large holdings in Argentina, Edward became an estate agent, and the daughter, Annie, married a lawyer, Harry Stephens, who was an eminently *safe* man.

John was the sole exception to this pattern, for he suffered a religious crisis as an adolescent and found himself unable to accept orthodox Christianity and its presumed social and economic corollaries. As his mother's diary reveals, his failure to follow the family's ways and to find a respectable, profitable mode of life was a source of concern, even pain, to his family, and Mrs Synge clung to the hope that John would find his way to God and would become more financially responsible.

Synge's brief 'Autobiography' gives us a selective account of his early development, laying emphasis on his interest in natural science and on the quality of his religious training, and, more implicitly, upon his sensitivity to the emotional tonalities of experience. Particularly important are the accounts of his youthful terrors about damnation and Hell, and his crisis of faith upon reading Darwin. That crisis will be considered in another light later, but Synge's conclusion from it deserves quoting at length here:

> My study of insects had given me a scientific attitude – probably a crude one – which did not and could not interpret life and nature as I heard it interpreted from the pulpit. By the time I was sixteen or seventeen I had renounced Christianity after a good deal of wobbling, although I do not think I avowed my decision quite so soon. I felt a sort of shame in being thought an infidel, a term which I have always used as a reproach. For a while I denied everything, then I took to reading Carlyle, [Sir Leslie] Stephen and Matthew Arnold, and made myself a sort of incredulous belief that illuminated nature and lent an object to life without hampering the intellect. This story is easily told, but it was a terrible experience. By it I laid a chasm between my present and my past and between myself and my kindred and friends. Till I was twenty-three I never

met or at least knew a man or woman who shared my opinions. Compared with the people about me, compared with the Fellows of Trinity, I seemed a presumptuous boy yet I felt that the views which I had arrived at after sincere efforts to find what was true represented, in spite of my immediate surroundings, the real opinion of the world.[5]

The emphasis here is upon the shame and consequent alienation that Synge felt at finding himself unable to believe. He felt this as a defection, as a betrayal of his family, especially his mother. But as Edward M. Stephens points out, Synge was caught in a dilemma, for while he was expected to agree with his family's religious beliefs, he also had been taught by his mother to be honest with himself and to seek the truth in all things. Statements of Synge's dilemma appear *passim* in Stephens' Typescript, but nowhere more clearly than in the following passage: 'When he was first overwhelmed by doubt he reserved judgment, but he could not avoid a decision. The conflict was latent in the religious system that he had accepted. He had been taught the virtue of faith, and at the same time the virtue of an honest search for truth. His mother had told him that the Protestant faith was free from superstitution, and depended on 'The Open Book' and the use of private judgment. She had often repeated, 'Seek and ye shall find, knock and it shall be opened unto you' (Matt. VII: 7). His research appeared to be disclosing facts contrary to his faith. The dilemma seemed insoluble' (TS, p. 250). So Synge's adherence to one of his family's principles brought him into conflict with others, and there was no satisfactory way out. He could not by any force of will simply *believe*, and he began to feel the anguish of that worst of 'tyrannies on human kind,' that which 'persecutes the mind.'[6]

This dilemma deeply influenced Synge's development. His guilt over his inability to believe was not transient but chronic. It became something to be taken into account continually, both in his relations with his family and in his development of a world view. And while the young Synge could partially locate the sources of his anguish, there were factors at work that he could not consciously realize. One of these was his own temperamental inclination toward separateness, toward setting himself apart and seeing himself as alienated. He says that the reading of Darwin laid a chasm between himself and kindred and friends, and that until he was twenty-three he 'never met or at least knew a man or woman' who shared his opinions. But surely there were even

in the Dublin of the 1880's and 1890's other persons suffering
crises of faith. It is understandable that Synge found none of these
among his relations, but that he found none anywhere else, including the Royal Irish Academy of Music or Trinity College, tells
us more about Synge than about Dublin. Nowhere does this bent
toward withdrawal appear more clearly than in his strange conviction while still a youth of 'between thirteen and fifteen' (*CW*,
II, 9) that his unhealthiness should prevent his marrying and
having children. Synge refers to this as a 'curious resolution which
has explained in some measure all my subsequent evolution.' But
what he describes does not explain the resolution itself. The
alienation Synge felt about his doctrinal difference was perhaps
a justification of his withdrawal, but it did not entirely cause that
withdrawal.

Another factor implicit in this crisis is the undue importance
Synge was drawn into giving to conceptual belief, to doctrinal
agreement or disagreement. This was not of Synge's creating, for
it reflected the value placed upon doctrine in the Protestant
Christianity he was surrounded by. Such an attitude involves the
doubtful assumptions that the most important features of a
religion can be distilled into its concepts or doctrines, and that a
person can simply and meaningfully reply to such questions as
'Do you believe in God?' or 'Do you believe Christ was God?'
or 'Do you believe in the spirit?' This concern with doctrine
neglects the emotive and tonal aspects of religion, relegating them
to an inferior position, while questions of belief, largely because
they are clearer and more distinct, are elevated to primary importance.[7] But while Synge suffered from this emphasis upon the conceptual, he was not able to understand and come to terms with
it.

This was particularly unfortunate in Synge's case, since, as his
early writings and his emerging aesthetic theories show, he had
a strong sense of the tonalities of experience, and was struggling
to express their reality and importance (note, for instance, the
concern with mood in excerpt 'e' in *CW*, II, 349). The undue
emphasis upon doctrine in his family's intellectual milieu stymied
and distorted his progress in this struggle, and produced a tension,
almost a disjunction, between thought and feeling. This rivalry
between feeling and belief is expressed in many ways in his
aesthetic statements, and even after he had more successfully
formulated his own view of art, Synge continued to show an undue concern over issues of belief. For example, in Notebook 42
(1908), Synge says, 'All theorizing is bad for the artist, because it

makes him live in the intelligence instead of in the half sub-conscious faculties by which all real creation is performed.' Another passage in the same notebook expresses the tension be-tween feeling and dogma when Synge speaks of the 'quite modern feeling for the beauty and mystery [of] nature, an emotion that has gradually risen up as religion in the dogmatic sense has grad-ually died.' Stephens points out that among Synge's early verses is one 'asking why he must interrupt his pleasure in nature by thinking' (TS, pp. 730-31). But Synge was not anti-intellectual: 'No one is less fond of theories and divisions in the arts than I am, and yet they cannot altogether be gone without' (Notebook 47). What Synge was working toward was not the banishment of abstractions, but their proper subordination to an emotive unity. Synge's struggle with the disjunction between thought and feeling was his own personal analogue of the 'dissociation of sensibility' affecting the culture at large, but Synge had no consoling aware-ness of this.[8]

Synge loved his family and wished to be loved by them, but their deep and irreconcilable differences of opinion muted the love they should have shared. The resultant supression of feeling by requiring conformity of thought spread to other areas of Synge's personality and caused him simultaneously to overvalue and to distrust abstractions. Conversely, Synge's fascination with strong emotions (remarked by Yeats and others) stems in part from his admiration of the simple, unequivocal state of being that such emotions express.

iii

There was, in spite of its relative neglect by critics, a deep affinity between Synge and his family. While he rebelled against their doctrines, he shared with them certain basic attitudes, even about religious issues. And the family continued to provide his main social context. In view of its importance to Synge's develop-ment, this social and religious milieu deserves our attention.

The people that Synge associated with from youth onwards were to a great extent members of the family. From the time he was a young child he was surrounded by relatives. His earliest companions in his explorations of the countryside were his brothers and his cousin Florence Ross. Synge never attended a boarding school, and his poor health dictated that most of his education took place within his home. His religious training was provided by his mother and grandmother. The summers in Wicklow were no less family gatherings, for while outsiders were occasionally invited, the society consisted mainly of relatives. Of a lunch at Glanmore in the summer of 1883, Stephens says, 'For John it was a rare experience to sit at a long table with a large party of strangers, but they, like most of the people he met, were members of the family clan. The visit tended to deepen in his mind the early impression that his social life was to be found among his relations' (TS, p. 217).

During his years at Trinity College Synge continued to live at home, and his extra-familial contacts during this time were practically nil. Stephens even says that because of his relatives and family friends on the Trinity College staff, 'John's entering college did not expose him to fresh influences for his new surroundings seemed only an extension of his home environment. His tutor was his mother's first cousin [Anthony Traill]; Charlie Miller an old friend of his family managed the College Office, and Marshall, the chief porter (who carried the mace), had grown up on the Glanmore estate' (TS, p. 355). Synge's failure to form friendships at Trinity or at the Royal Irish Academy of Music approaches abnormality. While he obviously admired Sir Robert Stewart, the only person he seems to have cultivated was a violin maker named MacNeil, and their relationship was so slight that MacNeil is not even mentioned in the Greene/Stephens biography (though he is occasionally referred to in Synge's diaries and in Stephens' typescript). Stephens does refer to Arthur Warren Darley, another violin pupil of Werner's, as 'John's lifelong friend' (TS, p. 501), but this involves an exaggeration that is itself revealing, for Darley is mentioned once, in passing, in Greene/Stephens.

Synge did later live in various places in Europe and he retained a flat in Paris for several years. But even during this period, most of his year was spent under his mother's roof, either in Kingstown or in whatever summer house she had taken in county Wicklow. Only twice, for very brief periods, did Synge attempt to set up housekeeping in Dublin. Throughout his lifetime, his family's house, his mother's house, continued to be his home, and, as Edward Stephens says, 'His mother . . . never made him feel unwanted at home' (TS, p. 895).

For all his differences of opinion with them (and these seem rarely to have erupted into open argument, especially after 1893), Synge never became as close to anyone outside his family as he did to his brothers, his nephews, and especially his mother.

Though there were aspects of his personality and world view that they did not understand, they seem in other ways to have known him far better than anyone else, and to have accepted him more readily and more completely. He continued to share with his brothers and occasionally with his mother, and later with his nephews, some of the experiences that meant most to him – his walking and fishing in the hills and glens of Wicklow. His diaries, and more fully his mother's diaries and letters, frequently refer to his long jaunts or fishing trips with Robert or Sam or Eddie. On these trips it is unlikely that they talked about religion, politics, or art, but they were together for long periods doing things they mutually enjoyed, and there must have been some communion among them. John probably felt on these jaunts a kind of belonging that he felt nowhere else.

The only extra-familial relationship deserving notice in this context is that with Molly Allgood, whom Synge loved and presumably wished to marry. This relationship had aspects that remained puzzling. There is no doubt that Synge did love this young lady, even if somewhat adolescently. His letters to her show his capacities for jealousy, pettiness, and self-pity, so that Molly probably glimpsed a side of Synge that few outside the family saw.[9] The letters also suggest that Synge enjoyed complaining about their being separated, and that he enjoyed anticipating their meetings almost as much as being with her. He seems to have made more of their social differences and their director/actress relationship than he need have. He also showed trepidation about revealing their relationship to his family, but his mother seems to have accepted her fairly well.[10] The precise reasons for their failure to marry remain vague. It is hard to see any tangible factors that prevented this during the fall and winter of 1907-08, but Synge continued to dawdle in his search for a house, continued to talk of 'next week,' until his abdominal operation in May of 1908 provided a more concrete deterrent to their union. In any event, as close as their relationship was, it seems not to have eclipsed the deeper relationship Synge had with his family, especially his mother.

Synge's relationship with his mother was the most important of his life. Nor was this true simply during his childhood, for they remained close until her death, less than five months before his own. Her home was Synge's home, and she remained for him a pillar and mainstay, concerned continually about the state of his soul and of his body, praying for him and nursing him in his several illnesses. In letters to Molly after his mother's death,

Synge said, 'I cannot write much, I am very sad when I think of all my life and how endlessly kind and good she has been to me' (October 26, 1908; *Letters to Molly*, p. 294), and 'My going home now will be very sad – I can hardly bear to think of going to Glendalough House she was always so delighted to see me when I came back from a journey – I can't go on' (October 28, 1908; *Letters to Molly*, p. 296). Several weeks later he wrote, 'People like Yeats who sneer at old fashioned goodness and steadiness in women seem to want to rob the world of what is most sacred in it. I cannot tell you how unspeakably sacred her memory seems to me. There is nothing in the world better or nobler than a single-hearted wife and mother. I wish you had known her better, I hope you'll be as good to me as she was . . .' (November 9, 1908; *Letters to Molly*, p. 299).[11]

In his typescript, Edward M. Stephens several times contends that some of Mrs Synge's attitudes and traits of character deeply influenced John. Stephens refers in one place to Synge's having had 'an active imagination stimulated by his mother's religious devotion' (TS, p. 179), and later calls attention to two of her teachings that he believes to have been influential on Synge: 'first the belief that nothing is in itself too small for attention from the mind of God, and secondly that to dwell mentally in such revelation as may lighten the darkness of human understanding is a moral duty' (TS, p. 212). Stephens says that Mrs Synge's favorite text in support of the first was Matthew 10: 29: 'Are not two sparrows sold for a farthing? and one of them shall not fall on the ground without your Father,' and Stephens says, 'John's intense interest in birds gave the text a special force, and the uneventfulness of his life inclined him to accept the belief that small familiar things might be significant, while much commonly regarded as important might prove vapid and meaningless' (TS, p. 213). In elaboration of Mrs Synge's second belief, Stephens says that she dwelt upon the transfiguration, and 'She explained that the vision was necessarily transitory, that when it had passed the three apostles who accompanied Jesus had to come down from the mountain, and that for them the importance of the experience depended on their minds dwelling afterwards in the glory of what they had seen. From his infancy John had been told by his mother that the beauty of nature is a special gift to man direct from the Creator. It had seemed to him that he and his cousin [Florence Ross] had together, through their delight in the woods and fields, found a special revelation' (TS, p. 213). Pursuing this, Stephens points out that John's early study of nature was encouraged by his mother (TS, pp. 223-24). She seems to have seen in it not the seeds of scientific rationalism, but a means of knowing and enjoying certain of God's gifts to us. Thus Stephens contends that Synge's sensitivity to natural beauty, always regarded as a hallmark of his work, owes something to his mother's influence. Stephens even suggests that Synge's prose style derives in part from his mother's forthrightness, saying 'there was in his ordinary prose a realistic truthfulness which appears to owe something to her teaching' (TS, p. 345).

Another idea Synge imbibed from his mother was that our life and talents come to us as gifts from God, and that we must acknowledge them, be worthy of them, and employ them. For Mrs Synge, this manifested itself in religious belief and practice and in stewardship over material possessions. For John this concept was more complicated, and his notebooks show his wrestling with it. He seems particularly to have been interested in the idea that some persons might by nature be intended to be playwrights or actors, and that if so, their obligation was to develop their talents along those lines. Stephens quotes the following passage from one of Synge's Notebooks:

> The common idea of God, among religious people, is a Being supremely good, delighting in virtue and in nothing else. But, if God did, as is generally believed, make man in the state in which he now exists, and if He guides and directs humanity in the present moment, if He gave us our intellects, can we believe that He does not require us to use them? Did He give Shakespeare or Garrick their abilities and not intend them to write and act? If He gives us our minds it is clear to me at least, that He wishes us to use them. It is a sin not to do so, and a virtue to fulfill his wish. (TS, pp. 369-70).

This passage is a revealing expression of the complexity of Synge's response to his family's religious milieu. It begins coolly, almost archly, with the 'common idea of God among religious people,' and is punctuated with *ifs*, but in the penultimate sentence slips in Synge's own conjecture that God is the source of his mind and the supporter of his intellectual search. And the last sentence speaks seriously of *sin* and *virtue*. Synge's speculation that God's gifts might include the capacity to write or perform plays would of course have been anathema to his family, for they regarded the stage as a device of the devil. But here we see how Synge could take certain religious principles or attitudes from his mother, reject the content she had given it (i.e. that God wishes us to be orthodox believers and good stewards of our property), and replace it with a content more compatible with his own artistic aims (i.e. that God wishes us to think diligently, or to write or to act).

In this regard, one of his Notebooks contains an interesting passage:

> The whole duty of man is to use. The so-called creations of Art are not to be attributed to the artist, he merely uses a mind which he did not make. If a man thinks he has formed his character or his mind, by persevering attendance on virtue or by study, he is wrong, for he did not make his perseverance, or his mind or the thing which he studies. The more power a man may feel in himself the greater is his responsibility. Man has power to destroy but none to build. We may throw away our abilities our characters or our lives. No man can say that he has always done the best that he could. Greatness among men consists in throwing away as few opportunities as possible not in doing anything meritorious. We must not take neutrality as doing nothing and mark off actions good and bad at either side. Doing nothing is desperate evil. Perfection, or doing our best on all occasions, is the first neutral point, and there our obligations are fulfilled. Many men are good relatively none absolutely. Real good would consist in doing something more than is required of us, and is of course beyond the power of creatures.[12]

This so clearly expresses several orthodox Christian ideas about man's relation to God that we almost expect to find parenthetical reference to the supporting scriptural passages – Christ's parable of the talents (Matt. 25: 14-30) and his statement 'Why callest thou me good? there are none good but one, that is, God' (Matt. 19:17). Most obvious here are two ideas, first that man has not created anything, but is entirely dependent upon a prior creation, both in the material he works upon, and in the capacities he brings to bear on it; second that man has a duty to fulfill the potentials he has been given. Though the passage nowhere specifically invokes God, this is clearly Synge's own version of orthodox ideas. Again it illustrates that, while he has revolted from certain doctrines or contents of his family's religion, he has not strayed far from its underlying assumptions and attitudes.

As Edward Stephens puts it,

John did not differ in type from his kindred with whom he could not agree. While he rejected their religious teachings he adopted the fundamental principles of their Protestant philosophy, and applied in his dealings with them the methods which they advocated for dealing with the world. He did not engage in any self-assertive provocative talk nor did he open unnecessary theoretical arguments. When he differed from them on matters of faith he claimed the right to think for himself and applied the individualistic principle, which they supported by the text, 'Come out from among them and be ye separate.' (TS, p. 397).

iv

Another opinion common among Synge critics is that he cared little or nothing for any 'theoretical' questions, whether religious or political. Here again, as with the issue of his alienation from his family, there is an element of truth, but it has been misconstrued and exaggerated. This view of Synge as indifferent to theoretical questions is sometimes related to the picture of him as an a-dogmatic spectator, or is sometimes a presumed corollary of his call for 'realism' in art, the assumption being that Synge saw all generalizations as antithetical to realism. Much of this opinion originated with those who knew Synge personally and should, it seems, have been in a position to know whereof they spoke. For example, John Masefield said, 'He was the only Irishman I have ever met who cared nothing for either the political or the religious issue.'[13] Lady Gregory said that Synge 'seemed to look on politics and reforms with a sort of tolerant indifference. . . .'[14] And in the most frequently quoted and most influential (and superficial) statement of this sort, W. B. Yeats said that 'Synge seemed by nature unfitted to think a political thought, and with the exception of one sentence, spoken when I first met him in Paris, that implied some sort of Nationalist conviction, I cannot remember that he spoke of politics or showed any interest in men in the mass, or in any subject that is studied through abstractions and statistics.'[15]

These views necessarily influenced others who wrote on Synge without having known him personally. For example, Maurice Bourgeois, whose book was regarded as the standard 'biography' until Greene/Stephens appeared, says that religious belief had practically no influence on Synge, and he even refers to Synge's peculiarly non-religious attitude.[16] And this opinion forms an important part of the portrait of Synge offered in the Greene/Stephens biography, where David H. Greene presents Synge's religious interests as underdeveloped or almost totally absent. Of Synge's responses to the people on the Aran Islands, Greene says, 'Because religion, for example, was to him only an idle superstition, he was particularly insensitive to the part it played in moulding the facts, if not the fancies, of Irish rural life' (Greene/Stephens, p. 86). Greene further plays down these aspects of Synge's mind when he says 'There is certainly no evidence beyond his correspondence with MacKenna that he had ever really been interested in the subject which took up so much of Yeats' interest,' and 'One is tempted to conclude that he was not the kind of man to take anything but the world of the senses very seriously' (Greene/Stephens, pp. 169-70).[17]

In spite of the weight of this opinion, I am convinced that Synge was indeed sensitive to and interested in religious questions, and theoretical questions generally, and I suspect that most recent commentators have simply followed earlier leads rather than examining the evidence.

There are several types of evidence of Synge's religious interests. For one, there is the undoubted impact that the crisis of religious belief had on Synge as an adolescent. This is one of the main themes of the 'Autobiography,' and its effects are acknowledged by Greene and others. Are we then to believe that something so traumatic for him as a boy was trivial and beneath notice for him as a man? True, the burnt child dreads the fire, but we must ask what form that dread might take, whether indifference or supersensitivity. That Synge became indifferent toward belief would seem possible only if he were successful in fully 'rationalizing' his beliefs, or rising above the need to believe, and this he does not seem to have done.

There is considerable evidence in Synge's diaries and notebooks that he not only retained an interest in religion and philosophy, but that he held what must be called religious beliefs. And while these beliefs would never have satisfied his mother or his brothers – would doubtless have shocked and disappointed them – they are generally consistent with pantheistic or mystical modes of Christianity. As some evidence of his continuing interest in religious and philosophical questions, we might list some of the books that Synge either annotates in his notebooks or mentions in his diaries as having read. I list only those with some obvious religious or philosophical aspect, leaving aside the question of whether his reading of Goethe, Wordsworth, Blake, Rabelais, Montaigne, or Maeterlinck might not also have such interest. The books that Synge refers to include Herbert Spencer's *First Principles* and his *Principles of Psychology*, Darwin's *Descent of Man and Selection in Relation to Sex*, Henry Drummond's *Lowell Lectures on the Ascent of Man*, Sir John Rhys's *Lectures on the Origin and Growth of Religion*, Alfred Nutt's essay on *The Celtic Doctrine of Rebirth*, Annie Besant's *The Ancient Wisdom* and *Esoteric Christianity*, Madame Blavatsky's *The Voice of the Silence*, A. R. Wallace's *Miracles and Modern Spiritualism*, G. R. S. Mead's *Yoga*, Frazer's *The Golden Bough*, Laurence Oliphant's *Scientific Religion*, Catherine Stevens Crowe's *Night Side of Nature*, Jules Bois's *Satanisme et Magic*, Jasper Niemand's *Purposes of the Lord, The Works of Jacob Boehmen, The History and Life of the Reverend John Tauler*, Swedenborg's *Heaven and Hell*, various recurrent readings in Locke, Hegel, Spinoza, Nietzsche, and Marx, and frequent readings of Thomas à Kempis' *The Imitation of Christ*. The list is not complete, but it should suffice to show that Synge was indeed interested in religious issues.[18]

While several of these books are simply listed by Synge in his diary as being read, others are summarized or annotated in his notebooks and were obviously read with care. To cite one rather out-of-the-way example, Synge digested some of the sermons of the fourteenth-century German mystic, the Reverend John Tauler. Synge's notes include the following:

> The pleasures of life come and go but we must *not set our affections thereon*. God takes a thousand times more pains with us than the artist takes with his pictures. Quotes 'Prayer is nothing but the going up of the soul unto God.['][19]

Given the contentions that Synge was uninterested in religion and that he aspired to rationalism, it is surprising for him to seek out the sermons of John Tauler, and doubly so for him to be copying down comments about prayer and the going up of the soul to God. This passage is also interesting and typical in another way. Here as elsewhere in Synge's annotations of such texts, he shows interest in ideas that have an aesthetic application; he seems in effect to be constructing an aesthetic, clarifying for himself what the artist is and what he does, and to be doing so in religious terms. While this does not confirm Synge's orthodoxy, it does show the kind of interest in religion we would expect from an aspiring artist who takes those matters seriously, and it shows that he was not indifferent or insensitive to religious issues.

There are similar and more detailed statements in the notebooks or in early drafts of plays, most of them in effect notes toward an aesthetic, that show even more clearly the religious tincture of Synge's thought. Consider the following:

> The emotions which pass through us have neither end nor beginning, are a part of eternal sensations, and it is this almost cosmic element in the person which gives all personal art a share in the dignity of the world.
>
> *   *   *
>
> The world is a mode of the Divine exaltation and every sane fragment of force ends in a fertile passion that is filled with joy. It is the infertile excitements that are filled with death. That is the whole moral and aesthetic of the world.
>
> *   *   *
>
> Neglect nothing, for God is in the earth and not above it. In the wet elm leaves trailing in the lane in autumn, in the deserted currents of the streams, and in the breaking out of the sap, there are joys that collect all the joy that is in religion and art.
>
> *   *   *
>
> In nature is the art of God and unless our souls are godly enough to produce an art more beautiful than nature . . . it is better to be silent.[20]

I cite these passages not to illustrate a particular point about Synge's aesthetic, but to establish that he was interested in religious ideas and took them seriously. These and other passages are given a place in Synge's thoughts about art by William Hart in his essay on 'Synge's Ideas on Life and Art' (see footnote 20). There Hart describes Synge's view of life as 'emotive, pantheistic, evolutionary and tragically joyous,' and he says pointedly, 'Thus for Synge Art is because Nature is because Man is because God is' (p. 44), putting God squarely at the base of Synge's world view and his aesthetic.

It seems, then, that although Synge was not an orthodox Church of Ireland man, he did retain an interest in and sympathy toward religious questions. While he cast aside the doctrinal content of his family's belief, he did not cast aside many of the underlying attitudes and assumptions. E. R. Dodds was probably right when he said that one thing Synge and Stephen MacKenna shared was 'an unresting curiosity about the secrets of religious experience.'[21]

There is analogous evidence about Synge's attitudes toward politics. Lady Gregory qualifies her statement about Synge's political indifference by saying, '. . . though he spoke once of something that had happened as 'the greatest tragedy since Parnell's death,' '[22] A political interest several times surfaces in the articles Synge wrote about the 'congested districts' for the *Manchester Guardian* in 1905. In the essay entitled 'Possible Remedies,' Synge says, 'one feels that the only real remedy for emigration is the restoration of some national life to the people. It is this conviction that makes most Irish politicians scorn all merely economic or agricultural reforms, for if Home Rule would not of itself make a national life it would do more to make such a life possible than half a million creameries' (*CW*, II, 341, 343; see also Price's long footnote on pp. 283-284 which in part counters Yeats's famous statement about Synge's political indifference).

When Synge went to Paris, he joined the Irish League which Maud Gonne had founded, and David Greene says that he was an 'active' member, acknowledging that 'his lack of interest in politics has been greatly exaggerated' (Greene/Stephens, p. 62). When he later resigned from the League, he wrote Maud Gonne a letter explaining his reasons. There he said:

> . . . You already know how widely my theory of regeneration for Ireland differs from yours and most of the other members of *Jeune Irlande*.
>
> I do not wish to enter the question which of us may be in the right, but I think you will not be surprised to hear that I cannot possibly continue to be a member of a society which works on lines such as those laid down for the *Irlande Libre*. I wish to work in my own way for the cause of Ireland, and I shall never be able to do so if I get mixed up with a revolutionary and semi-military movement.
>
> I have considered the matter very carefully, and I see there is no course open to me but to ask you to take my name off your list of members. If you think well I shall be glad to attend your meetings in a purely non-official capacity, but that is for you and the committee to decide. As member I should have henceforth to contend every point raised in reference to the

journal (wasting your time and creating disunion) but as spectator I can still help you where and whenever it is in my power and for the rest keep an uncompromising silence (from Greene/Stephens, pp. 62-63).

I have quoted this letter at such length because in addition to showing Synge's interest in Ireland's cause, it contains some interesting implications for the question of his attitude toward matters of 'opinion' generally. The consensus has it that Synge was indifferent to such matters; Yeats said that for Synge other writers 'did not exist,' and that Synge was the man the literary movement needed, 'because he was the only man I have ever known incapable of a political thought or of a humanitarian purpose.'[23] Doubtless Synge's taciturnity and habit of withdrawal from conversation encouraged this opinion of him among others, and he developed a reputation for an ironic diffidence and an unassailable self-confidence. But the letter to Maud Gonne suggests something different: his resignation from the *Jeune Irlande* resulted not from his indifference to matters of opinion and principle, but from his being so concerned about them that the situation presented him with an unavoidable ethical choice – either compromise his principles or resign. This sounds more like extreme concern for one's principles rather than lack of interest in them. The problem was that these principles mattered so much for Synge that he found it difficult, almost impossible, to enter into free and open debate about them. Yeats or Joyce would have welcomed the chance to proclaim their ideas in public, to debate them openly, and not because they held their opinions lightly, but because they had a self-confidence and exploratory freedom toward them that Synge did not have. Was his taciturnity, his habit of being the observer, a result of supreme self confidence, or of fear of entering the lists? The phrase that ends his letter to Maud Gonne is significant: he wishes to keep an 'uncompromising silence'.

It was apparently a habit he had developed quite early. Consider this statement by Mrs Synge in a letter to Robert:

I see no sign of spiritual life in my poor Johnnie, there may be some, but it is not visible to my eyes. He is very reserved and shut up on the subject and if I say anything to him he never answers me, so I don't know in the least the state of his mind – it is a trying state, very trying. I long so to be able to see behind that close reserve, but I can only wait and pray and hope. (quoted in the Typescript, p. 325).

Here again we see the facade that Synge showed to so many, but in this case we have some evidence about what lies behind it. Does it reflect indifference? More likely it hides anguish, for this letter was written on April 16, 1888, Synge's seventeenth birthday, and the time, according to the 'Autobiography,' that his religious crisis was at its height.

This withdrawal into taciturnity may be another instance of his mother's influence. After Synge's religious defection came into the open he and his mother rarely argued about it or even discussed it. As her diary and the Stephens Typescript show, her typical pattern of response to an emergent argument (once she had become convinced that no change of mind was forthcoming) was simply to decline to talk about it. No one could attribute this to her lack of concern with the issues; it stemmed rather from her fear of the divisive forces that argument might loose, and her wish to maintain some degree of communication. In a letter to Molly about her relationship with Miss Horniman, Synge advises her to be 'steadily polite' and says 'One gets into the way of wearing a sort of mask after a while, which is a rather needful trick' (*Letters to Molly*, p. 139; May 22, 1907).

This evidence suggests that Synge had a deep, almost obsessive concern for the truth and for the integrity of his own mind and thought – that far from being indifferent to opinions, he was too deeply and fearfully concerned about them. Earlier I disagreed with Masefield's contention that Synge cared nothing for the political or religious issue. Masefield made another observation about Synge that seems more perceptive and that carries implications rather contrary to the first: 'He eschewed all things that threatened his complete frugal independence and thereby the integrity of his mind' (Masefield, *John M. Synge*, p. 27). This, I feel, comes closer to the man – a deep concern for the integrity of his mind and a wish to keep at a distance anything that threatened it. Synge was not unconcerned about matters of opinion; rather, he was too deeply concerned.

Some comments by Stephen MacKenna, the man who perhaps knew Synge best, who saw behind the facade more than anyone else, are appropriate in this regard:

'I judged S. [Synge] intensely, though not practically, national. He couldn't endure the lies that gathered round all the political movement, flamed or rather turned a filthy yellow with rage over them, gently hated Miss Gonne for those she launched or tolerated, loathed the Gaelic League for ever on the score of one pamphlet in which someone, speaking really a half truth, had urged the youth of Ireland to learn modern Irish because it would give them access to the grand old Saga literature; I have never forgotten the bale in his eyes when he read this and told me "That's a Bloody lie; long after they know modern Irish, which they'll never know, they'll still be miles and years from any power over the Saga." I have never known a man with so passionate, so pedantic a value for truth as S. He didn't so much judge the lie intellectually or morally as simply hate it – as one hates a bad smell or a filthy taste. This alone would put him off any public movement whatever.'[24]

Most interesting is MacKenna's statement that Synge simply hated the lie. While we must allow for MacKenna's flamboyance and intensity, the similes he uses and the vigor he attributes to Synge's own statements suggest a man for whom truth and falsity, i.e. 'opinions,' are of extreme importance. Edward M. Stephens also testifies to Synge's deep concern for truth: '. . . he hated anything in the way of a lie,' W. R. Rodgers quotes him as saying, and Stephens goes on to illustrate by telling of an incident out of his own childhood when Synge had given him 'a tremendous lecture on speaking the truth,' after he and his brother had compromised a promise they had given Synge. Rodgers comments that 'Synge's puritan upbringing put its mark on him permanently,' and speaks of his 'rigid regard for the truth.'[25]

In this connection, a passage from the 'Autobiography' is relevant. There speaking of his pre-college days, Synge says:

English literature also I read with much care though I was painfully conscious of my uncertain judgment and formed my opinions reluctantly for fear a blunder might lower me in my proper estimation. I believe I never allowed myself to like a book that was not famous, though there were many famous books, such as Tennyson's poems, that I did not care for. The Irish ballad poetry of 'The Spirit of the Nation' school engrossed me for a while and made [me] commit my most serious literary error; I thought it excellent for a considerable time and then repented bitterly. (*Coll. Works*, II, 13.)

This deep concern over holding the 'right opinion,' this fear of blundering, suggests that the young Synge felt a lack of self-confidence and an undue regard for correct opinions. And there is evidence that, while Synge came to the point that he could announce his low opinion of Tennyson or of the Nation school, he never was fully at his ease when debating such topics. Mac-Kenna says, 'Synge used to get, I remember, very angry when I disliked something which he liked; I think, however, he often accepted the adverse judgment, tacitly.'[26] While this illustrates a deep concern about opinions, perhaps even more striking is MacKenna's ascription of anger to Synge, for this is a side of Synge that almost no one else speaks of, at least no one beyond his family. His displaying such anger over opinions to MacKenna is evidence that he felt a closeness to MacKenna that permitted him to reveal more of himself than he usually did.

In place, then, of the usual ideas that Synge was an alien from his family, indifferent to religious or political issues and to matters of belief generally, I propose something very different. I suggest that while he could not accept his family's dogmas, he was in temperament and attitude quite close to them, and that in his own thinking he transmuted rather than rejected their religion. Further, for Synge matters of belief were not trivial, but traumatic. Far from being indifferent to opinions, Synge charged them with such importance that he could rarely be brought to talk about them openly and freely, and he was almost obsessively concerned with loyalty to the truth. The view of Synge as perfectly self-confident and indifferent is, I believe, superficial and misleading. He did frequently withdraw into himself; he did often assume the mask of the passive observer; he did keep his own counsel. This resulted not from indifference or self-confidence, however, but from an underlying timidity and lack of self-confidence on his part which nothing fully explains, and from an abnormal concern for opinions and beliefs, stemming in part from the emphasis upon doctrinal issues in his background. He may have seemed to Yeats and others a man solid and secure, maintaining an ironic, disdainful stance toward the petty concerns of the world, but the truth seems to lie in an almost opposite direction.

Since my purpose here is not to retell Synge's life story but to develop certain ideas necessary for understanding Synge's Aran Islands experience and the resultant themes in his drama, I shall simply glance at his years at Trinity College (1888-1892). I have already noted that he lived with his mother during his entire university career, and that he made no important social contacts through the university. He seems to have given little to his university studies and to have gotten little from them. Trinity College records indicate that Synge's performance there, especially during his first three years, was minimal – he kept only those terms he was required to keep to stay in the university, and his grades were often bare passes.[27]

During his final year, however, he found some subjects that interested him more, and he did better in them. That year he took Hebrew and Irish, and he applied himself enough that he win prizes, albeit modest ones, in both.[28] During this year he also pursued a growing interest in Irish antiquities, which meshed with his study of the language, but seems to have stemmed more directly from antiquities he saw on his long walks in Wicklow. Among the books he read at this time were William F. Wakeman's *Handbook of Irish Antiquities*, George Petrie's *The Ecclesiastical Architecture of Ireland*, and William Stokes' *The Life and Labours in Art and Archaeology of George Petrie*. As David H. Greene points out, Stokes prints some of Petrie's notes on the antiquities and people of the Aran Islands, and since Synge did have an uncle who had earlier worked there, these may have caught his fancy and attracted him to the islands even at this early time. Greene rightly says that Synge may have 'owed more to his college course in Irish than he was later willing to admit' (Greene/Stephens, p. 28). It did give him a start in the Irish language, it gave a new dimension to his walks through Wicklow, and it may have interested him in the islands that eventually played so important a role in his development.

One reason Synge gave so little time to his Trinity College work was that during the whole of this period he was also a student at the Royal Irish Academy of Music. For several years he put considerable time and energy into musical composition. His failure to follow music as a profession probably had several sources. His family felt that he lacked true talent;[29] he seems to have found solo performances almost impossible; and his deeper aspiration to write began to assert itself. But his long study of music was no fluke. Recent critical discussions have followed up hints in his notebooks and in drafts of his plays, showing that music entered strongly into his aesthetic theories and into his compositional aims.[30] One reason for Synge's interest in music was that it offered him an opportunity to deal in almost pure feelings or emotions, separated from conceptual concerns. I have already suggested that the family's insistence on dogmatic accord overemphasized the conceptual and denigrated the tonal aspects of experience and that it caused a rivalry, a division, between thought and feeling. Music provided a respite from this and a balance against it. In playing his violin, Synge could immerse himself in feeling; in his aesthetic theorizing, music gave him experiential justification and a vocabulary for articulating the tonal aspects of his works and for balancing these elements against the more simply conceptual.

Synge received his degree from Trinity in December 1892. The following spring he came to know his cousin Mary Synge, who was a concert pianist and music teacher. She strongly encouraged Synge in his musical career, and it was largely at her behest that he went to Europe in July, 1893, to pursue his musical studies. During the years 1893-1898, Synge made five trips to Europe, staying mostly in Paris or in Germany, but travelling to Italy as well. In Europe he met a number of people and came under a variety of influences. He soon abandoned music as a profession in favour of romance philology, though this was probably a cover for his true aspiration to write, rather than criticize, literature. In April of 1895 he began taking courses at the Sorbonne, including one from de Jubainville 'sur la civilization irlandaise comparée avec celle d'Homer' Greene/Stephens, p. 72), and in April of 1897 he attended a lecture by Anatole Le Braz on Brittany which excited him and initiated his study of Breton lore. In December of 1896 he met W. B. Yeats, who purportedly advised him at that time to go to the Aran Islands, which he did in May of 1898.

The period from 1893 to 1898, dominated by his several visits to Europe and the influences he found there, was an important phase of Synge's development, superseded only by the Aran Islands experience that began in 1898. Here again there is some critical consensus about the importance and the meaning of the European experience for Synge, but once again I am sceptical of the consensus. It is generally held that this was a truly important and formative experience, largely because it gave Synge an opportunity to escape the provincialism of his Dublin background, to talk with people who were not scandalized by his religious scepticism, and to develop a 'rationalistic' outlook. Robin Skelton goes so far as to say that the day of Synge's arrival in Coblenz 'was as much a turning-point in his life as that day when he discovered Darwin and found himself spiritually and intellectually as far from his family as he was now to become physically.'[31] But this exaggerates the importance of the European experience, just as an emphasis upon rationalism distorts it.

Before discussing this, however, we should consider a concurrent episode which illustrates the forces that Dublin subjected him to that he probably hoped to escape in Europe – his frustrating and fruitless courtship of Cherrie Matheson. Though relatively little is known about the relationship, it appears that Cherrie refused Synge's proposals primarily because of his un-orthodox religious attitudes. We do know that the Mathesons were a very religious family, Mr Matheson being a leader of the Ply-mouth Brethren sect. Synge had met Cherrie at Greystones and had come to know her better when her family moved into a house near his in Crosthwaite Park. But their differences of opinion seem to have cast a shadow over their relationship from the beginning. David H. Greene says:

> She was not unduly oppressed by her father's strict discipline and ascetic creed, but she accepted them nevertheless with un-questioning faith. It soon became apparent that she would never form any real intimacy with a man who could not assure her and her father that he believed in salvation. Synge seems to have sensed the hopelessness of the situation from the very beginning, though he did not admit it for a long time. (Greene/Stephens, p. 36).

Synge pursued his love for Cherrie with varying degrees of intensity for several years. When he went to Germany and met Valeska von Eiken, he apparently confided to her his romance and its problems. Greene says 'When he told her about his love for Cherry (sic) Matheson and about how his unorthodoxy was separating them, she dubbed Cherry "The Holy One" ' (Greene/Stephens, p. 37). Apparently his first proposal of marriage was in a letter he wrote to her in June of 1896. He was refused. He made another attempt in October of 1896 but was again refused. Mrs Synge wrote to Robert:

> Cherry came in this morning and is quite decided that she could not be joined to one of his opinions, and she says that she is awfully sorry, poor little girl, at all the trouble she has un-intentionally brought on me. I suffer more than she does. . . . He looks in misery since Cherry was here. . . . Johnnie has spoken quite openly to Cherry, and she is quite shocked and says that he is much worse in his views than he was when he went away last autumn. (Greene/Stephens, p. 55; ellipses are in Greene/Stephens).

Even after this Synge seems to have asked his mother to speak in his behalf, but this too failed and Synge left for Paris, appar-ently aware that their differences of religious belief posed an in-superable barrier to their union.

Though the evidence is not conclusive, it appears that Cherrie refused Synge because of their religious differences.[32] If so, this is another illustration from Synge's life of the power beliefs can have and the anguish and alienation they can cause: his love for a girl he several times proposed to was frustrated by their differences of belief. The episode also testifies to the importance Synge must have given these matters. Had Synge been indifferent to religious issues, could he not have done as so many others have and compromised his beliefs for the sake of love? Stephens tells us that he had an example close at hand. Discussing John's inability to dissemble, Stephens says 'His cousin Alec, when arranging to marry Daisy Graves, had feigned the religious devotion necessary for obtaining her mother's consent, but John hated deceit of any kind' (TS, p. 781). That he could not follow his cousin's example is further evidence that for Synge 'opinions' did indeed matter very much. In his frustrated love for Cherrie Matheson, Synge again experienced the truth of Dryden's lines he had earlier copied: 'Of all the tyrannies on human kind/The worst is that which persecutes the mind.'

There is little question that Synge went to Europe with great expectations, and that he hoped to find there something very different from what he left behind. David H. Greene points out that in October, 1893, when Synge had been in Europe for some three months, he thanked his cousin Mary for 'bringing him into a world he never knew existed' (Greene/Stephens, p. 37). He was especially pleased to be 'living among people who regarded music as an important profession and who accepted his ambition quite naturally' (ibid.). The comment typifies the contrast Synge found between Dublin and the cities of Europe – a contrast, largely, between provincialism and cosmopolitanism. That Synge felt he was breathing a new and more sophisticated atmosphere is also suggested by a comment his mother made in her diary: 'I had a long letter from poor Johnnie. He has a bad cold. Curious letter attributing his unsociableness to his narrow bringing up and warning me! I wrote to him, [but] did not say much on that subject' (Greene/Stephens, p. 37).

But the differences between Dublin and Europe turned out to be more apparent than real, and after the initial pleasure and disorientation that any traveller feels, Synge found himself in a social and intellectual atmosphere not very different from what he had known in Dublin. It must, for example, have been disappointing indeed that he failed to escape from the restrictive social mores of Dublin as fully as he had first supposed. Among his joys on first arriving in Germany were the young girls of the von Eiken family, and especially the youngest, Valeska. His diary for July 30, the day after his arrival in Oberwerth, says simply 'The day of Valeska' (Greene/Stephens, p. 37; the phrase is in Irish). The ease and spontaneity of their relationship is indicated by David H. Greene's comment 'She nicknamed him "Holy Moses," from an oath he used, and he called her "Gorse". Synge's relationship with this exuberant young girl must have been one of the main pleasures of his early days in Europe, and must have presented a strong contrast to the guarded, circumspect social relations he was accustomed to. Greene says, 'With Valeska, who would have shocked his mother, he talked openly about himself in a way he had not done since childhood with Florence Ross' (Greene/ Stephens, p. 37).

But if Synge believed he had found a different world, one freed from the social restraints that had fretted him in Dublin, he was soon to be disappointed. In January, 1894, he left Oberwerth for a stay in Wurzburg. The only person he knew there was a young lady he had met in Oberwerth, and he wished to visit her. First, though, he wrote to the von Eikens to ask about the propriety of it. David H. Greene tells us, 'Both Emma and Claire replied to him in separate letters that his caution was well taken. Claire wrote, "In Germany it is just the same as in England – no gentleman visits a lady," ' and Greene concludes, 'It was apparent to him that life with the von Eiken girls in Oberwerth was going to be difficult to duplicate in another city' (Greene/Stephens, p. 38).

This damper to Synge's hopes to find an open society was followed by a severer disappointment in January of 1895, when he learned that not even Oberwerth and Valeska provided the Eden he thought he had found. By this time Synge had known and corresponded with Valeska for fifteen months. He had confided to her the problems he was having with Cherrie Matheson, and she responded, 'If you want to unburden your heart about the Holy One I shall keep your secret. Let your *ordinary* letter follow soon and look into the future with confidence and trust in God' (Greene/Stephens, p. 45). Synge wrote as she suggested, but his letter must have overstepped the bounds of propriety, for her reply began 'Dear Holy Moses, who begins his letter with a "slip of the pen" and just writes "Dear Valeska" without adding "Miss" to it. What do I think of it? You see, Monsieur Moses, for this your friend has not given you permission, so in the next letter please don't make the "slip" again' (Greene/Stephens, p. 45). Since

Synge's letter to Valeska has not survived, we cannot know whether she was offended by the minor matter of the salutation, or whether the letter offended her in some other way. The point, however, is that Synge had thought he had found someone to commune with, had confided to her, and had been rebuffed. His reply, most of which is printed in Greene/Stephens, only thinly veils his disappointment and hurt. The final paragraph says: 'Unfortunately I shall only see you very little from now on and even then only for a very short time. And in the meantime you want me to write nothing but stupid compositions about the weather. Such a thing would have surprised me when I was younger. Oh yes, do as you please. Don't mind me!' (Greene/Stephens, p. 47).

It is true that Synge openly argued religious questions with some of the people he met, and this could never have happened within his society at home. But these discussions were not, I suspect, as radical or as rationalistic as critics have been wont to infer. One of his intellectual companions was Marie Antoinette Zdanowska, an art student who was a devout and articulate Roman Catholic. Another was an English girl named Hope Rea, who styled herself a rationalist, but who might more accurately be described as sceptical and exploratory, and whose subsequent letters to Synge reveal her sympathies with theosophy. She later joined the Theosophical Society.

Synge has been described by several persons, including some who knew him, as a rationalist, but I believe that the term had little more than metaphorical application to Synge. By 'rationalist' we generally mean one who believes in the validity and sufficiency of human reason to describe reality, who sees no need to posit any mystery about any aspect of reality, and who will not accept religious texts or authorities as valid sources of evidence. While the last term here may apply to Synge, the other two do not. He may indeed have gone through a time when he, in Wordsworth's phrase, 'drag[ged] all precepts, judgments, maxims, creeds, like culprits to the bar' (*Prelude*, XI, 294-95), but I do not think it went on for long. For, as we have seen above, especially in the passages quoted from his Notebooks, Synge was too aware of the mystery behind all things to regard reason as definitive, too sympathetic to the interplay of natural and 'supernatural' in our experience to try to draw any exclusive lines, too concerned with those tonal aspects of reality which rationalism denigrates. Doubtless he did wish to bring 'reason' to bear on some religious and ethical issues – to point out the inconsistencies between his family's religious beliefs and their social and financial practices –

but this should hardly qualify him as a 'rationalist'. Stephens says, 'His active mind was unable to accept contradictory ideas, and he struggled for consistent beliefs. He would have been quite unable to pray for "peace on earth and good will to men," while planning to evict poor Mayo farmers from their wretched mud cabins. Decision about religion seemed a pressing necessity, but nowhere could he find the repose of a sure faith' (TS, pp. 366-67). But as we have seen, Stephens presents Synge much more as a sincere if frustrated religionist than as a rationalist. Neither socially nor intellectually, then, did Synge find in Europe anything significantly different from what he had found in Dublin.[33]

The questions of the intellectual effects of Synge's European visits and of his rationalism are so subtle that they cannot be fully appreciated except through comparison with the later effects of his Aran Islands experience. We know in retrospect that Synge's European visits, however important they may have been in smaller ways, were not the mind-fertilizing experience that his sojourns on the Aran Islands turned out to be. While he was in Europe his literary aspirations did more clearly announce themselves, and he did during that time write poems, draft plays, and attempt a novel, but the work that he wrote between 1893 and 1898 was derivative and mediocre and would never have seen the light of day had he not written his later works. But as Synge's critics generally acknowledge, something happened as a result of his Aran Islands experience that permitted the release and expression of the genius which had so long lain dormant and well concealed.

We should now consider the event that was the beginning of Synge's intellectual pilgrimage, his reading of Darwin. We looked earlier at the shame and alienation that reading produced, but we lacked then sufficient context to appreciate how fundamental and paradigmatic that experience was. Properly understood as a crisis of *perspective* producing a *shock* of awareness, this event can be seen as the nucleus of all that we have considered so far. Within it lie the reasons why the European trips were relatively unfruitful for Synge and why his sojourns on the Aran Islands were revelatory. Further, Synge's reactions to the reading can be seen to contain the seeds for themes and devices that he cultivated throughout his dramatic career.

Synge tells us:

Before I abandoned science it rendered me an important service. When I was about fourteen I obtained a book of

Darwin's. It opened in my hands at a passage where he asks how can we explain the similarity between a man's hand and a bird's or bat's wings except by evolution. I flung the book aside and rushed out into the open air – it was summer and we were in the country – the sky seemed to have lost its blue and the grass its green. I lay down and writhed in an agony of doubt. My studies showed me the force of what I read, [and] the more I put it from me the more it rushed back with new instances and power. Till then I had never doubted and had never conceived that a sane and wise man or boy could doubt. I had of course heard of atheists but as vague monsters that I was unable to realize. It seemed that I was become in a moment the playfellow of Judas. Incest and parricide were but a consequence of the idea that possessed me. My memory does not record how I returned home nor how long my misery lasted. I know only that I got the book out of the house as soon as possible and kept it out of sight, saying to myself logically enough that I was not yet sufficiently advanced in science to weigh his arguments, so I would do better to reserve his work for future study. In a few weeks or days I regained my composure, but this was the beginning. Soon afterwards I turned my attention to works of Christian evidence, reading them at first with pleasure, soon with doubt, and at last in some cases with derision. (*Coll. Works*, II, 10-11).

The experience described here is, for all its intensity, not unusual: an enquiring young mind – one taught to search for truth – learns that science challenges and destroys some of his more dearly held religious beliefs. But the ordinariness should not be allowed to obscure certain interesting if implicit points. Edward Stephens glimpses one of these when he says, 'It seemed to John that the foundation on which her [Mrs Synge's] system of belief rested had been destroyed by the meaning that Darwin gave to familiar facts' (TS, p. 249). As Stephens suggests, Darwin did not give Synge new facts, so much as he gave him a new way of looking at things he already knew. This is manifested in the specificity and rapidity of Synge's response. Almost instantaneously, familiar facts were cast into a new pattern, and the new perception gave a palpable shock. It is as if the reading of Darwin provided the last reagent needed to produce an instantaneous precipitate. Synge says, 'My studies showed me the force of what I read.' The *data* of these studies was already with him, so that the reading of Darwin simply provided a new viewpoint on information he already had. Once the new frame of reference was suggested, it demanded a review and revaluation of much that the boy already knew. It was indeed as if a whole new body of information had been opened up to him, while in actuality he was only looking at old facts from a new perspective. And the effect, as Stephens puts it, was that he now 'first felt the *shock* of knowing that for him doubt was possible' (TS, p. 321; my italics).

We have seen several examples of the power of ideas in Synge's life. We saw it in his implicit valuing of doctrine and the tension this set up between his thoughts and his feelings; we saw it in the anguish he felt over his inability to accept his family's dogmas; we saw it in his loss of Cherrie Matheson because of his inability to feign agreement with her family's ideas; we saw it in his resignation from *Jeune Irlande* when he could not accept its principles. But nowhere does the power of ideas appear more tangibly or significantly than in this early, paradigmatic experience – in the *shock* Synge received as the implication of Darwin's ideas unfolded. Such a shock or dissonance is unpleasant, threatening, frightening, and the natural reaction is to search for ways to ease the tension, to reconcile the contradiction.[34] But Synge was caught in a dilemma that prevented any easy solution. Taught to search for truth, he could not, in order to preserve orthodoxy and familial harmony, simply ignore what Darwin had shown him. Once again, though he could not then have realized it clearly, he was suffering the tyranny of the mind – he was caught in a true intellectual dilemma and was victimized by the ideas swirling around him. He began to read works of Christian evidence, of science, of philosophy, in a search for some fuller understanding, some better ideas, to relieve the dissonance he felt. His European experience was in part a pursuit of this approach. He turned to scientism and rationalism and found there ideas that accorded with Darwin and with natural science generally, but those ideas failed to answer his family's orthodoxy and to do justice to his own religious thoughts and sensibilities. This early experience with Darwin and the realizations that followed upon it were too basic and went too deep to be corrected simply by acquiring new facts. What was needed was a new attitude, a new perspective, perhaps another shock of realization complementary to the first.

We see then why Synge's experiences on the continent and on the Aran Islands were of such different value to him. The underlying reason was that the modes of thought he found on the mainland differed in degree but not in kind from what he had known in Dublin. In Europe he may have met some new ideas, but he found no new perspectives. On the Aran Islands, however, Synge found a world view, a frame of reference so different from the one he had been reared in that it was like breathing a new atmosphere. The effect was not only to entice him to ideas and attitudes that had until then been latent in him, but to waken him to the power and the arbitrariness of any set of received ideas. Through this he found also a new impetus and a new self-confidence for his writing.

Yeats quotes Synge as saying, 'Is not style born out of the shock of new material?'[35] If we realize that by style Synge means a writer's total mode of expression, and that 'new material' provides the most palpable shock when it is familiar material cast in a new perspective, we can see the relevance of Synge's comment to his Aran Islands experience. Yeats also says of Synge that 'He had to undergo an aesthetic transformation, analogous to religious conversion, before he became the audacious, joyous, ironical man we know.'[36] This transformation was made possible by Synge's experience on the Aran Islands.

To appreciate the impact of this experience on Synge, we must recognize two things. The first, which we have been exploring in this chapter, is his state of mind when he went to the islands, a state characterized by his alienation from his family's orthodoxies, by an intolerable separation between thought and feeling, and by his loss of Cherrie Matheson – in general by his victimization by ideas. The second is the culture he found on the Aran Islands, a culture so archaic that, even at the turn of the twentieth century, it had not yet been infiltrated by the 'common sense' and rationalism of modern western thought. His stays on these islands gave Synge access to a mode of thought, perhaps even a mode of perception, sufficiently different from what he had known in Dublin or found in Europe that it generated another perceptual shock, complementary to the one earlier given by Darwin, but this one liberating rather than constricting. Here Synge found a culture whose received ideas and perceptual sets were qualitatively different from those prevailing in Dublin or Paris. He found a world view that had largely escaped the impact of the main currents of Western thought since the rise of the scientific method, and that had never fully succumbed to the rationalistic aspects of Christianity.

On these islands, then, Synge found release from his dilemma in two ways. First, these people experienced reality without the dissociation of sensibilities, without even the guilt over orthodoxy, that had plagued him, and thus they provided a new, more holistic pattern of response to experience. Second, his realizing that their perspective on experience was qualitatively different from his own prompted Synge to consider how variable and arbitrary the assumptions, the received abstractions of a culture are. Had he grown up here, rather than 150 miles to the east, many of the problems and dilemmas he had suffered from would never have arisen. Though we need not choose between them, this second influence of the islands was probably more important to Synge than the first, For though he did envy and emulate the wholeness of the people's response to experience, Synge could not become one of them. His experience on the islands served not to make him into a primitive, but to permit him, standing between the two cultures as he did, to see how large a role 'perspective' plays and how arbitrary and incomplete any single view of reality is. It was this awareness more than the primitive attitudes *per se* that enabled his plays and that determined many of their themes and devices. But before we can turn to the plays we must give fuller attention to the questions of the 'archaism' of Aran Island culture, and of what Synge's prose writings reveal about his experiences on the islands.

NOTES TO CHAPTER I

1. David H. Greene and Edward M. Stephens, *J. M. Synge 1871-1909* (New York, 1959). This work will be cited as Greene/Stephens. On the relationship of this book to my other main biographical source, Edward M. Stephens' Typescript (cited as TS), see the Introduction.
2. David H. Greene, 'J. M. Synge – A Centenary Appraisal,' in Maurice Harmon, ed., *J. M. Synge Centenary Papers* (Dublin, 1972), p. 180. This lecture also appeared in *Éire-Ireland*, VI, no. 4 (Winter 1971), 71-86.
3. I doubt that Masefield knew him well and shall question some of his statements about Synge. For all their myopia about his professional life, some members of his family 'knew' Synge better than did any of his friends. A good discussion of Synge's relationships with several persons is Ann Saddlemyer's 'Synge and Some Companions, with a Note Concerning a Walk through Connemara with Jack Yeats,' *Yeats Studies*, No. 2 (1972), pp. 18-34. Prof. Saddlemyer says that 'while he lived, [Synge] had been a somewhat troublesome enigma' (p. 19).
4. Alan Price disagrees, saying that 'Probably the most satisfying utterances about Synge are those by Yeats,' and 'Yeats's evaluation of Synge exemplifies again the fact that the great poets are also the best critics' (*Synge and Anglo-Irish Drama*, [London, 1961], pp. 51-68). Price, however, deals most with Yeats's statements about Synge's works, not his person-

ality. Balachandra Rajan says that 'what [Yeats] saw in his colleague [Synge] was what the profession of being William Butler Yeats allowed or equipped him to see' (in 'Yeats, Synge and the Tragic Understanding,' in *Yeats Studies*, No. 2 [1972], p. 74). Robert O'Driscoll develops a similar point in his 'Yeats's Conception of Synge,' where, for example, he says, 'Synge is a symbol in Yeats's mind' (S. G. Bushrui, ed., *Sunshine and the Moon's Delight* [Gerrards Cross and Beirut, 1972], p. 161).

5. From the 'Autobiography,' in *Collected Works*, II (London, 1966), 11. Subsequent reference to the *Collected Works* will be given as CW.

6. In his diary for 1893, in the February 19 entry, Synge has 'Dryden's Hind and Panther Part I. Of all the tyrannies on human kind/The worst is that which persecutes the mind.'

7. This tendency is characteristic not only of Protestant Christianity, but of Western thought generally. The emphasis upon beliefs rather than attitudes, even the presumption that the doctrines can be separated from the experiential context of a religion, is an example of what A. N. Whitehead has called the 'fallacy of misplaced concreteness,' i.e. presuming reality to reside somewhere other than where it does reside. A recurrent theme of Whitehead's philosophy is that we should give higher regard to the tonal aspects of experience than we do. In pursuance of this, Whitehead challenges the assumption of Descartes, Locke, and Hume that the most fundamental factors of experience present themselves most clearly for analysis (see the essay 'Object and Subjects' in *Adventures of Ideas*). Whitehead's metaphysic often presents fascinating analogies with the aesthetic theories of Yeats and Synge.

8. The quotations from the notebooks can be found in volume II of the *Collected Works*, pp. 347-51. What Synge was striving for is Keats's Negative Capability – 'that is when man is capable of being in uncertainties, Mysteries, doubts, without any irritable reaching after fact and reason' (letter of Dec. 21-27, 1817).

9. The *Letters to Molly* have been edited by Ann Saddlemyer (Cambridge, Mass., 1971). In a letter of July 20, 1906, Synge berates Molly for having walked with Dossy Wright and complains, 'As for your excuse you are as well able to keep on your feet as any one I know, and even if you weren't a sprained ankle is a trifle compared with what you have made me suffer' (*Letters to Molly*, p. 6). Similar complaints can be found in letters on pp. 3, 29, 61, 73, 216, and 229.

10. For indications of Mrs Synge's reaction to Molly, see pp. 79, 108, 189 of *Letters to Molly*.

11. One strange feature of their relationship was Synge's being away during her death and burial. When he left for Germany on October 6, 1908, his mother was already ill, and in a letter to Molly from Coblenz on October 20, he said, 'I am very sad tonight as I have just got very bad news of my poor old mother – she is much worse I am afraid – if she does not soon get better I shall have no one in the world but you – one's brothers and sisters though mine could not be kinder – are never the same as one's mother or one's wife. I have a lump in my throat as I am writing – She is in bed again now too weak to read or write. Her life is little happiness to her now and yet one cannot bear the idea of not having her with us any more. If she gets worse I will go home, perhaps, very soon I do not like to think of her all by herself in the house' (*Letters to Molly*, pp. 291-92). Synge clearly regards her death as imminent, yet

says he may go home if she worsens! But he did not return for her death or for her burial. Probably he left and stayed away at this time because he was not willing to face the trauma of these events. Robin Skelton agrees, saying 'He must have known his mother was dying, but was not strong enough to face that crisis. Just as in the past he had avoided confrontations by telling both Samuel and his mother of his marriage plans by letter rather than face to face, so now he could not help evading the issue' (*J. M. Synge and His World*, [N.Y., 1971], pp. 123-24). Skelton also quotes the letter of November 9 and says, 'The loss of his mother affected him profoundly. She had been throughout his life a fixed and unwavering point of reference' (*J. M. Synge and His World*, p. 124).

12. From Notebook no. 3 (Trinity MS. 4371). In the foliation provided by the Trinity College staff, this occurs on ff. 42-43.

13. John Masefield, *John M. Synge: A Few Personal Recollections* (New York, 1915), p. 11.

14. Lady Gregory, *Our Irish Theatre* (New York, 1965), p. 123.

15. W. B. Yeats, 'J. M. Synge and the Ireland of his Time,' in *Essays and Introductions* (New York, 1968), p. 319.

16. Maurice Bourgeois, *John Millington Synge and the Irish Theatre* (1913), p. 181. See also pp. 218-19.

17. Greene touches on the question of Synge's sensitivity to religion again in his 'Centenary Appraisal,' but is less definite in his conclusion. See *Centenary Papers*, p. 194. Ann Saddlemyer speaks in passing of Synge's 'indifference to religion' (*Letters to Molly*, p. xvii). Robin Skelton devotes more attention to the issue in *The Writings of J. M. Synge* (Indianapolis, 1971), where he repeatedly speaks of Synge's rejection of Christianity and of his 'anti-clericalism'. And Seán MacMahon pursues the same tack in his ' "Leave Troubling the Lord God": A Note on Synge and Religion,' *Éire-Ireland*, XI (Spring 1976), pp. 132-141.

18. Many of these works are referred to or summarized in Notebook 10 (MS. 4378) or Notebook 11 (MS. 4379). The former was 'mostly used during the period 1898-9,' the latter 'probably dates from 1894-5' (See *The Synge Manuscripts in the Library of Trinity College Dublin*, [Dublin, 1971], pp. 40-41.

19. These unpublished notes are in Notebook Eleven (MS. 4379). For the sermon that Synge is annotating, see *History and Life of the Reverend John Tauler*, trans. by Susanna Winkworth (London, 1857), pp. 211-17. It is Sermon V, the Sermon for Epiphany. The underlining is Synge's own, and he fails to close the quote.

20. The first three passages are found in *Collected Works*, III, pp. 174, 168, and 164 respectively. They are statements by Colm in *When the Moon Has Set*, but they clearly reflect Synge's own ideas (R. Skelton says that 'Colm is too obviously a vehicle for the author's opinions' – *Writings of J. M. Synge*, p. 18). The last passage is from Notebook Fifteen and is quoted in William Hart's 'Synge's Ideas on Life and Art,' *Yeats Studies*, No. 2 (1972), p. 45.

21. Dodds' statement occurs in the 'Memoir' preceding Stephen MacKenna's *Journals and Letters* (London, 1936), p. 11.

22. Lady Gregory, *Our Irish Theatre* (New York, 1965), p. 123.

23. W. B. Yeats, *Autobiography* (New York, 1965), pp. 347, 384.

24. Quoted from a letter to Arthur Lynch in *Journal and Letters of Stephen*

MacKenna (London, 1936), p. 39. In a letter in the *Irish Statesman* of October 20, 1928, Lynch said, 'The man who knew him [Synge] best was Stephen MacKenna.' Lynch's letter is reproduced in part in MacKenna's *Journal*, p. 11.

25. W. R. Rodgers, *Irish Literary Portraits* (London, 1972), p. 96. Stephens recounts the episode referred to on pp. 1436-37 of the Typescript. He also tells in the Typescript of another form Synge's probity took – his refusal to undermine with his own unorthodoxy the religious training the young Stephens boys were receiving from Mrs Synge.

26. *Journals and Letters of Stephen MacKenna* (London, 1936), p. 12.

27. In his Typescript, Stephens shows that when Synge took his entrance exams for Trinity, he had the idea of going for the prize in composition and of going for honors in literature. He was dissuaded by his poor grades on the exams, and by the fact that his poor handwriting would count against him in his essays. This suggests that Synge had literary aspirations much earlier than is generally thought (TS, pp. 316, 343, 356-57).

28. See *The Dublin University Calendar for the Year 1893*, pp. 125-27, for details on these prizes. A comparison of the amounts distributed for the prizes with the amounts Synge received, and Synge's low position on the non-alphabetical list of recipients, are the basis of my judging his prizes to be modest.

29. In a letter to his brother Robert, dated September 6, 1890, Samuel said, 'We all feel that Johnnie is not very wise in going in so hard for music, as, for *one thing* among several reasons, he is not very musical we think, although very fond of it. I can't say either that he plays well, at least as yet. I think that perhaps he is better at the composing than at the playing. I don't know if you know that at present Johnnie is thinking of taking up music as a profession and giving lessons on the violin. In time he might be able to do something that way, but I think he would find it not very satisfactory' (letter in packet #3 [1890] of Mrs Synge's letters to Robert, Trinity College Collection). In a letter to Max Meyerfeld of September 1, 1905, Synge himself said, 'I saw that the Germans were so much more innately gifted with the musical faculties than I was that I decided to give up music and take to literature instead' (*Yale Review*, July 1924, p. 698).

30. See especially two essays by Ann Saddlemyer, ' "A Share in the Dignity of the World," ' in *The World of W. B. Yeats* (Seattle, 1965), and 'Art, Nature, and the Prepared Personality,' in *Sunshine and the Moon's Delight* (Gerrards Cross and Beirut, 1972).

31. Robin Skelton, *J. M. Synge, and his World* (New York, 1971), p. 29.

32. Greene draws his information from Mrs. Synge's letters and diaries and from Cherrie Matheson's memoir that appeared in the *Irish Statesman*, July 5, 1924, pp. 530, 532, 534. The memoir is of limited value, since Cherrie says that she did not meet Synge until late 1896 or 1897 (which diaries and letters disprove), and she makes no reference whatever to any love between them or to proposals of marriage. More recently Ronald Ayling has rediscussed the relationship, but the only new information he has consists of letters from Cherrie's children about their mother's relationship with Synge, and general information about Kenneth Houghton, later Cherrie's husband. Ayling, drawing directly on the opinion of Cherrie's daughter, concludes rather loosely that their union

was prevented both by Cherrie's lack of love for Synge and by their religious differences ('Synge's First Love: Some South African Aspects,' *Modern Drama* VI [1964], 450-60). The spelling *Cherrie* follows Ayling, who says that, according to her son and daughter, she herself spelled it that way (Ayling, op. cit., pp. 456-57).

33. I see some evidence for this in Synge's describing Huysmans as 'sick with monotony trying to escape by any vice or sanctity from the sameness of Parisian Life' (*Coll. Works*, II, 395).

34. The term 'cognitive dissonance' has come into use in recent years to refer to the state of mind produced when basic life-beliefs or deep seated assumptions about reality are challenged. The idea has some appropriateness to Synge's situation. See Leon Festinger, *A Theory of Cognitive Dissonance* (Stanford, Calif., 1962); Jack W. Brehm and Arthur R. Cohen, *Explorations in Cognitive Dissonance* (New York, 1962); and Leon Festinger, *Conflict, Decision, and Dissonance* (Stanford, Calif., 1964).

35. W. B. Yeats, *Autobiography of William Butler Yeats* (New York, 1965), p. 358.

36. W. B. Yeats, *A Vision* (New York: Macmillan, 1961), p. 167.

II
The Verge of the Western World

Appreciating the kind and degree of influence the Aran Islands had on Synge requires familiarity with his state of mind when he went there and with the culture he found there. Chapter I considered the former; this chapter explores the latter. Chapter III will bring the two together by examining *The Aran Islands* to see what features of Aran culture most attracted and affected Synge.

I believe that Synge found in the islands a culture that deserves to be called archaic. This claim consists of two parts – first that Celtic culture is characterized by attitudes not typical of the Western mind, and second that such attitudes could have survived and been available at the turn of the twentieth century. It is helpful to distinguish these two points here at the outset, but it will be difficult (and unnecessary) to keep them separated as the discussion progresses. The word *archaic* itself implies both aspects of the idea – both primitive, pre-Western perspectives, and the strong conservatism of Celtic culture, its capacity to perpetuate itself, to survive in the presence of challenging elements. In developing these points, I shall whenever possible use examples relating to religion or to the Irish language and oral tradition, because these are so intimately involved in the question of archaic survivals, and because they were of special interest to Synge and will be relevant to points later in this study. We should, for example, keep in mind the question of the relationship between Celtic paganism and Roman Catholicism, and we should note the recurrence of the idea that language has the power to affect reality. Both of these become issues in Synge's plays.

The question of whether twentieth-century Irish culture may have preserved an archaic leaven is relevant not only to understanding J. M. Synge, but to appreciating certain strands of Anglo-Irish literature. Anglo-Irish literature is distinguished from modern European or American literature in part by its having succumbed less to some intellectual currents that have dominated recent Western thought. The problem that modern writers have inherited is how to heal the schizophrenic division between mind and body, subject and object, that is our heritage from scientific empiricism and Cartesian dualism. Scientific empiricism implies that only those things that can be weighed or measured are real, and Descartes, hoping to save the realm of spirit from the incursions of this new methodology, proclaimed two substances, mind and matter. But Descartes' intention backfired, resulting in a severe split between matter and spirit and in doubt about the very existence of thinking substance.

Irish writers such as Yeats, A. E., Lady Gregory, or O'Casey were aware of this, but they were less severely affected by it than modern writers generally, partly because of the presence in their cultural milieu of certain pre-scientific or archaic attitudes. As a result, the Irish writers more readily and more frequently affirm the Imagination – i.e. a power blending mind, body, affections – while other writers are debilitated by, or expend their energies in struggle with, the autonomy of the intellect and the division of mind and body. The Irish were not of course the only advocates of holism: [1] Lawrence protests man's over-emphasis on the intellect; Eliot depicts our dissociation of sensibility; Stevens' continual theme is the Imagination. The Irish writers, however, do seem to have found it easier to retain a sense of the potential wholeness of experience, of the reality of moods and of the tonal aspects of experience; they kept something of the modes of perception that prevailed before the new philosophy cast all in doubt, or before 'the new conception of law', as Synge calls it, came about.

The archaism of Irish culture has been much discussed in recent decades. Several knowledgeable scholars have argued that Irish culture, largely by virtue of Ireland's insular position off the Western edge of Europe, has retained many features from earlier periods of history or pre-history. Much of the research and argument has gone to show that early Irish literature, law, and social structure reflect conditions traceable to the Indo-European phase of Western history, before the differentiation and development of Greek and Roman cultures.

Among the most valuable sources of evidence are the early Irish law tracts. In his important lecture on 'The Linguistic and Historical Value of the Irish Law Tracts' (1943), D. A. Binchy argued that 'Irish law preserves in semi-fossilized condition many primitive "Indo-European" institutions of which only faint traces survive in other legal systems derived from the same source.'[2]

Though most of his time is spent in showing the linguistic conservatism of these texts, Binchy also points out several parallels
between the early Irish customs and those found in Hindu society,
stemming from a common Indo-European or Aryan source. He
says that 'The parallelism between the Irish and the Hindu law
books, both of them the work of a privileged professional class,
is often surprisingly close: it extends not merely to form and
technique, but occasionally even to diction' (Binchy, p. 215).

The specific analogies between Hindu and Irish institutions and
customs that Binchy points out are of interest, but more
important to our purpose are two underlying principles that he
discusses. The first is the great conservatism of Irish culture:

> The conservatism which philologists have often noted as a
> feature of the Irish language is paralleled in Irish law, and
> largely for the same reason. Between the Goidelic conquest
> and the Norse invasions Ireland remained insulated from the
> impact of foreign peoples and institutions, in other words from
> the most powerful factors making for legal change. Above all,
> it never came within the political and administrative frame-
> work of the Roman Empire. It is true that, following the intro-
> duction of Christianity, Roman law came to exercise an in-
> direct influence upon Irish law; but such accretions can easily
> be recognized and separated from the body of native custom.
> The antiquity of the latter has already been noted by several
> legal historians. Indeed, the writings of the Irish jurists are
> something more than a faithful record of the customs of the
> conquering Goidelic tribes: they also furnish detailed informa-
> tion about certain early institutions which are but dimly
> reflected in the most ancient records of cognate legal systems.
> (Binchy, p. 213).

The second principle, suggested in this passage and more specifically invoked elsewhere in the lecture, is the capacity of the Irish
traditions to exist intact, or at least discernibly, beneath an over-
lay of other quite different, more typically western, influences.
Binchy's suggestion that the Roman 'accretions' can easily be
distinguished and separated from 'the body of native custom' is
again drawn on in his comparison of Irish with Welsh law. Of
these he says,

> Even their points of difference are instructive; for these throw
> light on the extent to which Welsh law had been 'modernized'

by its reception of Roman legal ideas, institutions, and terminology. The outstanding difference between them is the prominence which the Welsh 'codes' assign to the State, as represented by the king, in matters of private law, whereas in Ireland the more primitive system, under which there is no public enforcement of private obligations, still obtains. . . . In Ireland . . . there is no evidence of any such intervention by the 'State', and thus the written law shows all the conservatism and reverence for the past that characterized its professional custodians. When to this difference we add the fact that even the latest tracts were compiled at least two centuries before the 'code' of Hywel Dda, we can readily understand why Irish law has retained so many more primitive features than Welsh. (Binchy, pp. 215-16).

These same principles of conservatism and of ability to retain its identity beneath a foreign veneer underlie Binchy's discussion of the change, or lack of change, brought about by Christianity:

The one important external influence on the system came with the conversion of Ireland to Christianity. As in all other countries, the reception of the new faith was accompanied by alterations and innovations in the older law. Yet I think that most scholars have exaggerated the extent of the revolution it effected in Irish law. They have been unduly impressed by the wording of the tracts, which only received their definitive form after the law schools had long been Christian. . . . Nevertheless, beneath the Christian phraseology of the tracts, there lies a hard core of pre-Christian institutions, just as in Roman law the constitutions of the later emperors did little more than adorn with a façade of Christianity the essentially pagan structure erected by the jurists. Compared, say, with the Anglo-Saxon laws, the Irish tracts show, on certain fundamental points, an obstinate refusal to conform to Christian teaching. (Binchy, pp. 217-18).

Binchy goes on to discuss examples of how the traditional laws prevailed over the wishes of the Church. These include the regulations concerning transmission of property (the traditional jurists maintained a system that made bequests to the Church difficult), and regulations concerning marriage, which preserved the old Irish customs of various degrees of union and of concubinage.

In discussing this point, Binchy calls attention to another striking trait of Celtic culture – the dispersed, *tuath*-based structure of Irish society and he suggests that 'the main reason why Irish law was not completely Christianized lay in the absence of anything like a central authority which the Church could use, as it used the various Anglo-Saxon kings, for the purpose of introducing the necessary reforms' (Binchy, p. 218). This social and political structure is a characteristic of Celtic society, and it has acted as a conservative force. Until the coming of the Scandinavian invaders in the eighth and ninth centuries, Ireland had no cities and was organized politically into a loose grouping of petty kingdoms, with no central king. Likewise the Christian Church in early Ireland, instead of developing the efficient hierarchy that it did elsewhere, adapted itself to the loose Celtic scheme and became organized around many small and essentially separate monasteries. E. Estyn Evans, writing in 1957, said 'It is significant that even today no inland Irish town has a population reaching 20,000: in the Republic, indeed, only one or two exceed 10,000, and that barely. It is the immemorial peasant tradition which dominates the heart of Ireland.'[3] More recently Caoimhín Ó Danachair has pointed out that 'The Gaeltacht districts of today are populated by small rural communities of farmers and fishermen, without a single town, with scarcely a village of any size.'[4] And Evans points to the conservative inclination of such a culture, saying, 'Down to our own day the small size of the average farm has encouraged the survival of simple tools and limited the acquisition of machines. . . . The retention of many of the attributes of a peasant society is the key to the survival of the folk ways with which we are concerned in the following chapters' (*Irish Folk Ways*, p. 10). These conservative influences are, as we shall see, present in full force in the Aran Islands.

Another important contribution to this question was Myles Dillon's lecture 'The Archaism of Irish Tradition' (1947).[5] There he says pointedly,

> My purpose is to show that certain features of Irish tradition suggest that Ireland, on the margin of the Indo-European area, has preserved Indo-European characteristics that have been lost in most other regions of the west. It will appear that in social organization, in language, and in literature the peculiar character of the Irish evidence is due, not to the influence of a pre-Celtic substratum, as has sometimes been suggested, nor to drastic innovation, but to conservatism. (Dillon, 'Archaism,' p. 246).

Dillon draws on Binchy's earlier lecture and develops further the idea of the Indo-European origins of certain Irish customs and the parallels with Indian culture resulting from their common origin. He says, for example, that the Celtic druids and the Indian brahman shared not simply a common ancient vocabulary, but that 'they preserved common Indo-European traditions of practice and belief, some of which survived in the Gaelic world down to the eighteenth century and have survived in India to the present day'. (Dillon, 'Archaism,' p. 246). As an example of a social custoiл shared by the two cultures, Dillon mentions 'fasting as a means of enforcing legal claims'. ('Archaism,' p. 247).[6]

Equally interesting are a number of other similarities that relate to the power of language and the importance and persistence of the oral tradition in both cultures. One example Dillon discusses at some length is the 'Act of Truth, based upon a belief in the magic power of the truth'. ('Archaism,' p. 247). The essential trait here is a belief that the utterance of truth has some tangible power, perhaps to cause death, or to roast a pig, or to restore eyesight. Dillon says 'In Ireland as in India the notion of the magic power of Truth was familiar'. ('Archaism,' p. 251).

Dillon also discusses the similarity of the literary traditions, and their common Indo-European heritage:

> The form of Irish epic tradition is a prose narrative with occasional passages of verse, the verse being used for dialogue to mark any heightening of the mood: love, anger, death. This form appears in some of the most ancient Hindu writings, and both Oldenburg and Windisch have maintained that it is the earliest form of Indo-European narrative. ('Archaism,' p. 253).

And in addition to this similarity of narrative form, Dillon discusses 'specific *motifs* which support the theory that in India and in Ireland a common tradition has survived'. ('Archaism,' p. 255).

According to Dillon, 'the most remarkable resemblance between the literatures of India and Ireland is in the matter of bardic poetry'. ('Archaism,' p. 259). He discusses the several parallels between the Hindu *kavi* and the Irish *fili*. He points out that the training of the *fili* lasted for many years and that he was reputed to have various 'means of divination by means of which he could foretell the future or discover the truth'. ('Archaism,' p. 261). And the *fili's* ability to wreak havoc by his satire was acknowledged: 'The power of the *fili* rested upon fear of his displeasure, for just as he knew the art of praise, he knew also how to condemn in verse the victim of his anger, and his satire *(aer)* destroyed the honour of a prince and damaged his substance'. ('Archaism,' p. 261).

Dillon concludes his discussion by focusing an important question:

> May we then suppose that a common tradition persisted so long in these two peripheral areas? I suggest that we may. I am sure that it is the true explanation. Just as in the domain of language a common vocabulary survived in the names of king and priest and in words proper to the functions they performed, so in the domain of culture the social institution of court poets survived and developed on closely parallel lines. ('Archaism', p. 263).

Another study of interest to us is Kenneth Hurlstone Jackson's *The Oldest Irish Tradition: A Window on the Iron Age* (Cambridge, 1964), in which Jackson discusses the possibility that the early Irish epic, the *Táin Bó Cúailnge*, reflects an Iron Age culture. Briefly, the facts behind the question are these: the events that form the story of the *Táin* – the war between Connacht and Ulster for the brown bull of Cooley – were traditionally thought to be set about the turn of the Christian era, and there is evidence that such a state of warfare did exist between these two regions in the pre-Christian period of Irish history (i.e. pre-432 A.D.). However, writing was not introduced into Ireland until the coming of Christianity in the early fifth century, and the earliest probable date for the writing down of native material such as the *Táin* stories is agreed to be about 600 A.D. (Jackson, pp. 52-53). Further, the earliest surviving manuscripts of the *Táin* date from the twelfth century (Jackson, p. 52), and we can only guess about what manuscripts existed between about 600 and 1200. In order, therefore, for the *Táin* to reflect pre-Christian Irish culture, the stories would have to have been handed down through oral tradition for several centuries and have survived an unknown number of recopyings after being committed to manuscript. Given our contemporary view of the looseness and unreliability of oral and even of manuscript traditions, this seems improbable indeed.

But in the face of this unlikely situation, Jackson, a highly knowledgeable Celticist, argues that 'when all due allowance is made for later accretions the stories provide us with a picture –

very dim and fragmentary, no doubt, but still a picture – of
Ireland in the Early Iron Age'. (Jackson, p. 5). More specifically,
he says,

> It is obvious that the Ulster of the hero tales represents
> that kingdom before it was broken to pieces in the fifth cen-
> tury, and that these tales show us a polity of Ireland which is
> 'pre-historic' in exactly the same sense as the Mycenaean polity
> preserved in the *Iliad* is 'pre-historic'. This gives a most valu-
> able starting-point – the Ulster cycle represents a state of affairs
> older than the fifth century. This date is remarkably confirmed
> by other factors. (Jackson, p. 48).

In support of this claim, Jackson stresses the great integrity of
the Irish oral tradition and the respect in which it was held. He
concludes,

> To declare with confidence that it [the *Táin*] belongs to a
> period about the time of the birth of Christ, but that the stories
> were not written down till some 650 years later, stretches one's
> credulity rather far. Is it credible that a story-telling tradition
> could be handed on orally without very great change over such
> a vast period of time? Many people would think that it is not,
> and would scout any such idea. We must remember, however,
> that the early Irish *filid* and story-tellers were professionals who
> had had a rigorous training, part of which was aimed at perfect-
> ing them in this very thing, at memorizing and reciting and
> handing on a large number of traditional tales. It was their
> business and they were highly skilled at it. In such circum-
> stances stories may be passed on for centuries without any
> really fundamental change. I do not think, therefore, that it is
> at all extravagant to claim that a body of narrative first written
> down in the seventh century may have been formulated in, say,
> the fourth or possibly even earlier and handed on orally for
> 300 years or so by the professional Irish reciters in the way
> described. (Jackson, pp. 53-54).

If Professor Jackson is right, it shows a truly amazing archaism
and conservatism on the part of the culture, and an equally
amazing respect for the native Irish materials and for the tradition
of the word, both oral and written.

Synge was aware of and interested in such ideas about Irish
culture and literature, for while they have lately been more fully

substantiated, they are not recent discoveries. In his 1902 article on 'La Vielle Littérature Irlandaise', Synge said,

> J'ai parlé pluse haut de l'importance européenne de la littérature irlandaise et l'expression n'est pas exagérée. Dans nos légendes et dans les cycles dont je viens de parler, on trouve une mythologie qui forme avec la mythologie grecque de la première époque, un noyau de croyances les plus primitives que nous ayons des races indo-européennes. (*Coll. Works*, II, 354).

Synge also refers warmly to Alfred Nutt's study accompanying Kuno Meyer's translation of *The Voyage of Bran,* in which 'plusieurs questions relatives à la religion originaire des races indo-européennes, sont discutées avec soin, et le livre forme a chapitre extrêmement intéressant de la mythologie comparée.' He goes on

> Cette littérature est importante à un autre point de vue encore. La vie, les moeurs et les cultes qu'on y trouve dépeints ne sont autre chose que des phases de la civilisation de toutes les races celtiques de l'ouest de l'Europe au temps des Césars. Ainsi, en reconstituant le monde d'ou sont sortis nos textes, on arrive à se former une idée assez nette des anciens Gaulois.

The book Synge refers to, Nutt's essay *Upon the Irish Vision of the Happy Otherworld and the Celtic Doctrine of Rebirth* (London, 1897), is mentioned several times in his diaries and is annotated in Notebook Ten (MS. 4378) and it does contain discussions of the early Celtic legends and rituals stressing their archaic and Aryan character. While Nutt may not deserve comparison as a Celticist with Binchy, Dillon, and Jackson, Synge clearly knew such ideas and was influenced by them, as his many references to the archaism of Irish myth and literature show (see, for example, *CW,* II, 365, 366, 368, 370, 375).

The ideas we have surveyed about the archaism and conservatism of Irish culture have become quite widely accepted, so that we find the anthropologist R. A. S. Macalister saying that 'The importance of Ireland [is] that, thanks to the "time-lag", it has rendered to Anthropology the unique, inestimable, indispensable, service of carrying a primitive European *Precivilization* down into late historic times, and there holding it up for our observation and instruction.'[7] Similarly, E. Estyn Evans says that 'The outstanding interest of Ireland for the student of European origins lies in the fact that in its historic literature, language and social organization, as well as in its folklore and folk customs, it illustrates the marginal survival of archaic elements of the Indo-European world.'[8] It seems, then, widely agreed among authorities that Irish culture is highly conservative and that it did long preserve institutions and modes of Indo-European origin.

But even acknowledging this, it may seem questionable whether a culture that retained 'archaic' or 'prehistoric' or 'Indo-European' traits would have persisted to the turn of the century and have been available to Synge and to other Anglo-Irish writers of his time. It is often said that the death blow to the old Gaelic order occurred in the seventeenth and eighteenth centuries, with the vast 'plantation' carried out by Cromwell and the devastating penal laws that followed. E. Estyn Evans, however, suggests the general survival of archaic Celtic traits to a much later date when he says 'The retention of many of the attributes of a peasant society is the key to the survival of the folk ways with which we are concerned in the following chapters [of *Irish Folk Ways*]. Even the Great Famine which marks a grim watershed in social and economic history did not entirely obliterate them, though it had such far-reaching effects that it might be regarded as the end of prehistoric times in Ireland' (*Irish Folk Ways*, p. 10). As we shall now see, there is evidence that in certain isolated Gaeltacht areas, such as the Aran Islands, cultural practices and attitudes that deserve to be called archaic did indeed survive into the twentieth century.

In developing this point, I will occasionally cite evidence relating to remote areas of Ireland other than the Aran Islands. This seems appropriate, for the evidence about the Aran Islands is consonant with that from other such areas, and the consensus is that these islands present a culture equally as or more primitive than that anywhere in Ireland. I will also use Synge's works as evidence. This involves no circularity of argument, for *The Aran Islands* is, in addition to being our best guide to Synge's interests, a reliable picture of how things were.[9]

Since we are specifically concerned with the Aran Islands, we should first consider certain facts about their geography and their social and economic conditions in Synge's time. These facts, though simple, are impressive, for they make us realize how untouched by modern developments these islands were. This stems largely from their being difficult of access, and from geological and social factors that rendered technology virtually inapplicable, especially to the two smaller islands.[10] Not until 1891 was there a regular steamer service from Galway to the islands, and even then only the largest island, Inishmore, had a pier that could accommodate the steamer. The two smaller islands did have slips that could, when tides and weather permitted, accommodate a small trawler. Most of the fishing and transport of these smaller islands was, however, done by curagh, a small canvas and tar covered rowboat made by the islanders. For all the inhospitability of the elements, the islanders had to maintain a subsistence economy, for the use of the boats, from steamer to curagh, was dependent on the weather, and when it was bad the islands might be cut off for days or weeks. The islands are very rocky, and the islanders had over the years literally manufactured much of the soil from seaweed, manure, and broken-up stone. The main foods were seafood (usually salted) and potatoes, and some livestock were raised, partly for use on the islands, partly for sale. Some small income was gained from the sale of kelp (the burned down residue of a seaweed), valuable for its iodine content, and in earlier days the people had, using harpoons thrown from the curaghs, killed the huge basking sharks for their oil, though this stopped when paraffin became available. The people made their own clothing from local wool, and their shoes, called 'pampooties', from cowhide. The houses were of native stone, with roofs thatched with rye grown on the islands. Ownership followed the traditional 'rundale' system, by which one man might have four or five small fields scattered around the island.[11] These fields were often only a few hundred square feet in area and were separated by rock walls – no gates – which had to be taken down and re-built to gain access to the fields. The rocks come from the fields themselves, in apparently endless supply; some enclosed areas remain almost pure rock even today. All of these factors made modern technology, even the plough, useless, and Yeats hardly exaggerated when he referred to 'those grey islands where men must reap with knives because of the stones' ('Preface to *Well of the Saints*', in *Essays and Introductions,* p. 299). Roads on the islands were few and primitive, but they sufficed, since there were so few wheeled vehicles. There were as a matter of fact no wheeled vehicles at all on the two smaller islands, and Synge even tells us that on Inishmaan there was only one bit and saddle. All in all, then, we can safely say that the Aran Islands, especially the smaller two, were in Synge's day as uninfluenced by modern communication, transportation, and technology as any part of Europe, and that they differed little from what they had been a thousand years before.

The Irish language was one of the primary vehicles of the preservation and transmission of the early Irish cultural milieu, and there is a connection between the degree to which Irish is spoken and the degree to which the old ways are maintained. In the Gaeltacht, the old customs were more fully maintained than where English became the native language.[12] This is true partly because language is so integral to any culture, but it seems particularly true here, because so much of the way of life turned on language both as vehicle of history and literature, and as pleasure-yielding and perhaps even magically potent in itself.

Furthermore, the introduction of English into an area was especially likely to bring the demise of the old ways because of the modes and purposes of its teaching. The decline of Irish and the ascent of English in Ireland was not a case of a fair rivalry of languages along a linguistic border. As Douglas Hyde pointed out, 'This extinguishing of the Irish language has not been the result of a natural process of decay, but has been chiefly caused by the definite policy of the Board of "National Education", as it is called, backed by the expenditure every year of many hundreds of thousands of pounds.'[13] Hyde goes on to point out that the National Board insisted that even schoolchildren who knew no English were started out to read in that language, that the teaching of the Irish language, as of Irish history, was prohibited (*Lit. Hist.*, p. 633), and that the children were encouraged to think of themselves as English, not Irish.[14]

In view of this close connection between the survival of the language and of the older culture, the use of Irish on the Aran Islands in Synge's day should be noted. In his *A View of the Irish Language,* Brian Ó Cuív presents maps reflecting the linguistic situation in Ireland as revealed in the censuses of 1881, 1891, and 1961. According to the map for 1891, Irish was spoken by 80 percent or more of the population in only an extremely small part of Ireland. This consisted of one section of county Galway, and the Aran Islands. No other areas of Ireland had so great a concentration of Irish speakers. The pervasiveness of the language on the islands is also indicated by some comments of Douglas Hyde in his *Literary History of Ireland* (1889). He says that the Danish scholar Dr Pedersen, who had recently lived on the islands for three months to 'learn the language that is there banned', found that 'at the present moment the only inhabitant on one of these islands, not counting coastguards, who does not speak Irish is the schoolmaster!' (*Lit. Hist.*, p. 634, fn. 1). It seems clear, then, that, in the decade of the 1890s, Irish was spoken as fully on the Aran Islands as anywhere in Ireland, and that whatever influences the language exerted to maintain the old ways existed there in full force.

One important way the persistence of Irish influenced the survival of Gaelic culture was that it was the vehicle of the oral tradition. There are of course fine Irish story tellers who tell stories in English, but certain qualities of the oral tradition seem to have been regarded as untransferable to English. This was in part because of an almost mystical attitude that was commonly held toward Irish, which must be taken into account in any discussion of Gaeltacht culture, or of the effects of this language and culture on Synge.

We have already seen the respect, even reverence, that was accorded the *fili* in early Irish culture, and we have seen examples of the almost magical power attributed to language. Elements of this persist with the maintenance of the oral tradition even into the twentieth century. For example, the old fear of the poet's satire is seen repeatedly in Irish culture in the seventeenth to twentieth centuries. Douglas Hyde's play *The Twisting of the Rope* (1901) tells of the stratagems of a family to evict an unwanted poet from their cottage without incurring his wrath and his curse.

There is ample evidence that the oral tradition did continue in the Gaeltacht into the nineteenth and even the twentieth century. The last decade of the century saw the publication of several collections of folk tales collected from oral sources in the west of Ireland.[15] And Myles Dillon attests to an even later continuation of oral tradition on the island of Inishmaan. Arguing that the prose narrative with verse interpolations links Irish literary form with Hindu, Dillon, speaking in 1948, says, 'But in Ireland the form preserved in the *brahmanas* is the common saga-form. Indeed it can be said to have survived in folk-tales down to the present day, for I have heard a Fenian tale recited in Inishmaan with the speech of the hero in verse.' ('Archaism', p. 255).[16]

One important feature of the archaism of the Aran Islands' culture involves the people's attitudes towards the doctrines and mores of Christianity. This is particularly important for the points I am developing about Synge, because his family's religious orthodoxies were basic features of the frame of mind that I contend Synge escaped from on the islands. The problem, of course, is that these islands, as the whole of Ireland, had been Christianized since the fifth or sixth century, and the people were all Roman Catholic. It may then seem unlikely that the islands would afford Synge anything very different from what he knew in Dublin, except as Roman Catholicism might differ from evangelical Protestantism. What Synge found in the religious situation of the Aran Islands was, however, different indeed from what he had known at home.[17]

The main factors determining this difference we have already seen – they include the physical and political remoteness of the islands, the severe natural environment, and the impressive conservatism of Gaeltacht culture. But another factor comes into play here – an absence of dogmatism within the culture that seems more characteristic of the Eastern religious outlook than the Western.

Specifically, the religious outlook Synge found on the islands involved a strange blend of orthodoxy and unorthodoxy, of Christianity and paganism, and it involved a sympathy toward a wide range of 'supernatural' phenomena which would have struck any typical modern person as inconsistent and anomalous. This was true, moreover, not simply of the attitude toward specific doctrines or beliefs, but even of certain emotional reactions among the people that seemed contrary to orthodoxy, even to common sense and to logic. We shall see this more fully when we turn to *The Aran Islands,* where Synge repeatedly shows his fascination with the strange moods and emotions of the people.

The clearest example of this lack of dogmatism is the willingness of the people to believe in both Christian and pagan powers. The islanders were, of course, Roman Catholic, but they were also in many respects pagan, for they believed not only in Christ and in God's angels, but in the *Fear Darrig* and the *sidhe.* Synge's account of the islands contains (as we shall see) frequent references to the people's belief in fairies, and Daphne Pochin Mould confirms this through other evidence in the chapter 'The Gaelic Tradition' in her book *The Aran Islands.* Mould says, 'Belief in fairies was in Synge's time and later very real, universal, and sometimes dangerous'; to illustrate, she refers to the problems met by Nurse B. N. Hedderman, who worked on the islands:

For Nurse Hedderman, a few year later [than Synge], belief in fairies was a horrible reality. It was thought in Aran and elsewhere that fairies could and did steal children and replace them with changelings. In fact, Aran boys wore petticoats like their sisters, to deceive the fairies, until they were quite grown up. Nurse Hedderman had to fight this belief, for a sick child might change so much in appearance and personality that the parents would become convinced it was a changeling and be unwilling to nurse it. One such 'changeling', sick with whooping cough, recovered, and then the mother claimed that the fairies had restored the original child to her again.[18]

While the islanders believed in a God of mercy who loves and cares for his children – there is even a tradition that no harm can come to a curagh carrying a priest or curate[19] – they also knew that the sea is itself a powerful, severe deity, and they were willing to placate it by a variety of means. Alfred Nutt, in his essay on *The Celtic Doctrine of Rebirth* (which Synge read, and annotated) makes essentially this point:

> The peasant is alike credulous and sceptical, tenacious of old custom and largely tolerant to anything that appeals to his sense of logic. He will grant the efficacy of the Christian rite, especially when it is presented to him under the quasimythological guise of saintly influence, but he will not renounce the older practice; in dealing with powers so capricious as those of Nature, the wise man accepts all the help he can get; the saint may fail here, the fairy there, the witch in a third case, and where one fails the other may succeed. And the older powers he cherishes, in spite of priests and saints, are not the gods whom the imagination of poets and the ambition of priests had glorified, rather their ruder prototypes to whom all along his worship had been paid. . . . And whereas in every other European land the ministers of the new faith were as bitterly opposed to the fanciful as to the business aspect of the older creed, in Ireland it is the saint who protects the bard, the monk who transcribes the myth, whilst the bird flock of Faery, alike with the children of Adam, yearn for and acclaim the advent of the apostle. (*The Celtic Doctrine of Rebirth*, II [London, 1897], 204-05.

We are told that the conversion of Ireland from paganism to Christianity in the fifth and sixth centuries was relatively tranquil, that it was a bloodless conversion. One probable reason for this was that the Irish did not feel the necessity of making an either-or choice between Christianity and their native religion. They were willing to accept the God of Christianity as a supplement to, or an extension of, their native religion, rather than as a replacement of it. In this they reflected a tolerance that is 'Indo-European' rather than 'Western'. Christianity, under the influence of monotheistic Hebraism and of philosophic Hellenism, early came to regard its truth as unique and definitive, and took a dogmatic attitude toward it. The religions of India, stemming in part from Indo-European religion, have never taken on that attitude and an Indian sees no problem in 'believing in' several of the religions available to him. The native Irish culture had something of this same cast of mind, and the inclination to regard Christianity and the native attitudes as mutually supplementary rather than exclusive persists even into modern-day Gaeltacht Ireland. In her *Visions and Beliefs in the West of Ireland,* Lady Gregory says, 'I believe that if Christianity could be blotted out and forgotten tomorrow, our people would not be moved at all from the belief in a spiritual world and an unending life; it has been with them since the Druids taught what Lucan called "the happy error of the immortality of the soul".' (p. 15).

The ability to move easily between pagan and orthodox ideas was, as we shall see, one feature of island life that most strongly attracted Synge. And well it might, for in their a-dogmatism, in their ability to move without apparent remorse or guilt between supposedly contradictory or at least mutually exclusive world views, these people presented a direct contrast to what Synge had always known. We have seen that in his milieu belief was extremely important, and defection from the true belief had dire consequences – alienation, guilt, disjunction of thought and feeling. Here by contrast was an almost Edenic unconcern for such distinctions.

One example of the strong persistence of pagan custom and attitude, even under criticism from the Church, is the Irish wake. The wake is a custom that certainly goes back to pre-Christian origins – and is also one that seems inscrutable not only to Christian orthodoxy, but to modern common sense as well. And there is no doubt that the Church did find the customs surrounding the wake offensive and made attempts to eradicate it, or to bring it in line with more orthodox death rituals. In Seán Ó Súilleabháin's *Irish Wake Amusements,* the idea of a tension between native institution and the Church's wishes appears repeatedly, and he devotes an entire chapter to 'Church Opposition to Wake Abuses'. Ó Súilleabháin's discussion of the wake illustrates again our earlier points about the amazing conservatism of Irish culture, and the persistence of pre-Christian custom into the twentieth century. Ó Súilleabháin says,

> The waking of the dead is a very ancient custom throughout the world. Extant accounts of wakes in Europe go back almost a thousand years. The practice has died out, however, on most

of the continent of Europe within the past century. It still survives in Ireland and is likely to continue so for some time.[20]

Of more specific interest to us is Ó Súilleabháin's discussion of the Church's opposition to the wake. Ó Súilleabháin points out that

> . . . there were certain aspects of traditional wakes which drew down strong condemnation from the Irish Church. Bishops and priests made many attempts to curb the practices to which they objected; strong pastoral letters were issued from time to time in some dioceses, and bishops, on their visits to administer Confirmation here and there, preached against the abuses. Also when Synods of bishops of an archdiocese, or of the whole country, met, the Statutes issued by them concerning religious matters often included one dealing with wakes and funerals; the faithful were urged, or ordered, to discontinue certain traditional practices; the clergy were urged to see that the orders were carried out. This they attempted to do, as we know from many sources, through sermons and personal contacts down through the centuries. (p. 146).

In his small book, Ó Súilleabháin cites or refers to more than two dozen instances of ecclesiastical directions, injunctions, sermons, against the practice at the wakes (see especially pp. 19-22 and 146-57). Usually the clerical injunctions were against the unchristian or sinful practices of singing lewd songs or against suggestive or licentious actions, and the aim was to prevent sexual misconduct, which the Church would regard as sinful *per se.* But the objections were not always to such sinful activities. For example, frequently listed among the prohibited actions were any sort of hilarity on merry-making at the wake. Not of course that the Church objected to hilarity, but it did object to it at a ceremony for the dead, where the thoughts of the living should, presumably, be solemn. Ó Súilleabháin tells us that in the Synod of Armagh, August 23, 1670,

> Statute 2 ordered the clergy to have nothing to do with wakes or funerals, where sport and amusements were carried on by night in the wake-house – behaviour which was an insult to God and a scandal to a Catholic community. Parish priests who were negligent in endeavouring to end these abuses would be deprived of their parishes. (p. 147; Ó Súilleabháin cites Rev

Laurence Renehan, *Collections on Irish Church History,* Dublin, 1861, p. 158).

These passages deserve some scrutiny, for they contain interesting implications about the basis of the tensions between the Church and native Irish customs and they cast some light on the qualities of the Celtic mind that attracted Synge. As we have seen, some of the practices objected to were pernicious or sinful. But others were not – these others involve not sin, but an impropriety of emotion, a tendency to express (and presumably to *feel*) an emotion different than the Church finds appropriate. This concern for and disagreement over propriety of emotion is an interesting revelation of the basic difference between the Church's perspective and that of the native culture.

Christianity, reflecting a rational view readily accepted by most Western Europeans, deems that at a time of bereavement, we express sorrow, not hilarity. Hilarity at such a time suggests an emotional opacity, perhaps even a moral obtuseness, that offends our deeply ingrained sense of what is appropriate, and for this reason it is more than mildly disconcerting. But the point is that the Irish people apparently *felt* no such inappropriateness. They had to be told, and told repeatedly, that there was something indecorous about this.[21] They did not feel the same partitioning of emotions – grief and hilarity – that the Church wished them to feel, or that most rational people presumably feel. We have here a custom expressive of a mode of feeling and of thought that does not conform to the Church's or to reason's sense of what is appropriate. It expresses a culture that has never fully conformed to received, 'rational' modes of thought, and illustrates the native Irish culture's preservation of a custom and a mode of feeling that may appropriately be called pre-logical. This is not to say that there is no pattern, no inherent decorum, to this custom, but simply that the pattern it involves is so different from our own, that it surprises, even shocks us, and makes us feel that the custom is somehow deeply illogical.

The passages I have quoted also suggest the Church's unease and defensiveness about another expression of indecorum or illogic – the people's penchant for parody, or for 'mock-imitation of the sacred rites of the church' (p. 150). This tendency reflects a failure to see the seriousness and solemnity of these rites and to take the proper attitude toward them, or, put differently, a failure to take the received attitude toward them. In *The Irish Comic Tradition,* Vivian Mercier points to parody and burlesque as recurring modes of Irish humor, and he cites several examples, from the earliest manuscripts down to the present time. These modes of humor grow out of a refusal to conform to a received way of thinking or of regarding some ritual – something basically analogous to what we have seen in the attitudes reflected in the wake.

As another illustration of this point, consider the Church's strictures on another part of the wake, one that was severely objected to, but that can hardly be regarded as sinful or even as inappropriate to death – the keening of the dead. The keen (Irish *caoine*) is an ululating, moaning cry over the dead, some form of which has existed in many primitive European communities. Those who have heard it testify to its eerie, almost terrifying, effect. But it is an expression of grief and lamentation, and as such would seem an acceptable part of a death service. Yet the Church repeatedly objected to it and attempted to suppress it. Consider the following pastoral letter quoted by Ó Súilleabháin:

Diocese of Cashel and Emly
Sometime about the year 1800, Most Rev. Dr. Thomas Bray, Archbishop of Cashel, issued a pastoral letter which said:
'We also condemn and reprobate, in the strongest terms, all *unnatural* screams and shrieks, and fictitious, tuneful cries and elegies, at wakes, together with the *savage* custom of howling and bawling at funerals. And, in place of these *pagan* practices, so *unmeaning,* and so *unbecoming* Christians, we exhort all persons, who frequent wakes and funerals, rather to join, at the *proper* time, during the night and morning of the wake, with other *pious* persons, in fervent prayer, for the soul of the deceased: to comfort those that are in affliction, and in the interim also to meditate *seriously* on death, or otherwise to observe a becoming silence; shewing in their whole deportment a most edifying and sober gravity – which should always appear in every Christian on so awful an occasion, where the real image of death lies before his eyes.' (p. 140, italics mine; Ó Súilleabháin cites *Stat. Synod. Cassel et Imelac* [1813], 108–).

The words I have italicized highlight two things – that the Church regarded the keen as savage and pagan, and that it felt that it involved an impropriety or breach of decorum. But as we have said, the keen can hardly have been regarded as either sinful or as inconsistent with grief. Why then the objection? I suggest that it was mainly because of the inability of the clergy to fit the depth and range of emotion the keen expressed into their sense of what grief should involve. They did not fully understand what it meant, but they sensed that it was somehow antithetical or offensive to the Christian perspective. The churchmen felt a kind of 'cognitive dissonance' between the ideas of Christianity and the feelings the keen expressed, and they moved to relieve the tension by banning the keen.

One specific aspect of the keen troubled the clergy and incurred their criticism, and will probably trouble persons unfamiliar with the customs surrounding it. Most of us regard the keen as a strange but acceptable expression of deep grief, and we are probably amused by the intolerance of the clergy in attempting to suppress it. But even a sophisticated modern person may be disconcerted to learn that most of the keening was done by hired, professional keeners, and that there were persons who went from funeral to funeral and made their living as professional mourners. It was, in fact, common not only to hire such mourners, but to leave most of the immoderate mourning to them. And there are stories of various groups of professional keeners attempting to outdo each other in their keening.[22]

For most of us this knowledge produces a clash of emotions. Immoderate, savage grief, we may be able to accept; but we must be puzzled, perhaps offended, at the idea that the family could allow their dead to be mourned for hire. We are tempted to say, 'Don't they know what emotions are appropriate to death – don't they have any sense of decorum?' In short, we find ourselves in the position of the priests, or of anyone who encounters customs that are 'irrational'. But to the Irish people the hiring of mourners was an accepted part of their culture, neither monstrous, nor irrational, nor inappropriate.

My aim in this closing example has been to provide a small instance of that shock we often feel in encountering a culture different from our own. Unless we withdraw from such an experience and close our minds to it, it will show us how differently things may be done in other cultures, and make us aware that some of our most implicitly accepted ideas, perhaps even our emotional reactions, are not absolute or natural, but are socially conditioned. This awareness can in turn make us realize how pervasive a role our accepted ideas can play in our commonsense perceptions of our experience, and how different reality might look to us if we could get beyond our implicit preconceptions. What happened to Synge on the Aran Islands was precisely this realization.

NOTES TO CHAPTER II

1. Though *holism* remains the more usual spelling, I prefer *wholism* (a spelling recognized by *Webster's Third New International Dictionary*) since that form more immediately suggests the idea of unity.
2. The lecture was published in the *Proceedings of the British Academy*, XXIX (1943), 195-227. The quotation is from pp. 199-200.
3. *Irish Folk Ways* (London, 1957), p. 8.
4. Caoimhín Ó Danachair, 'The Gaeltacht,' in *A View of the Irish Language*, ed. Brian Ó Cuív (Dublin, 1969), p. 116.
5. Published in *Proceedings of the British Academy*, XXXIII (1947), pp. 245-264. Several of Dillon's points in this lecture are amplified in *The Celtic Realms*, by M. Dillon and Nora Chadwick (London, 1967).
6. See also *The Celtic Realms*, p. 99, where this point is developed more fully. It is interesting that when we think of fasting and of passive resistance as social or political device we think first of the Indian, Gandhi, and that our contemporary word for passive pressure – boycott – comes directly from nineteenth-century Irish history.
7. R. A. S. Macalister, *The Archaeology of Ireland* (London, 1949), p. x.
8. E. Estyn Evans, *Irish Folk Ways* (London, 1957), p. xiv.
9. As an index of its reliability, citations of *The Aran Islands* comprise six of the eighteen references in geographer R. A. Gailey's 'Aspects of Change in a Rural Community' (*Ulster Folklife*, V [1959], 27-34).
10. Here and in Chapter III I will several times allude to the differences between the largest island, Inishmore, and the two smaller ones, Inishmaan and Inisheer. We shall see that the latter were considerably less touched by modern technology, and that Synge preferred them because they were more 'primitive'.
11. One policy of the Congested Districts Board to modernize Gaeltacht Ireland was the replacement of the rundale system by more efficient 'striping,' which consolidated each man's holdings. Robin Flower testifies to the great impact this had when he says of the Great Blasket that, largely because of the institution of striping, the aspect of the island had changed more in the few years he had known it 'than in all the previous years of its existence' (*The Western Island* [New York, 1945], p. 39).
12. Seán Ó Súilleabháin says 'Had Irish remained the normal everyday language of our people, it is probable that storytelling in that language would have survived fairly normally even up to this age of mass communications. But the coming in of English almost put an end to storytelling, as the tales never passed over, in any but a very small degree, to the new language. The curtain has now almost completely fallen on what was once one of our people's main sources of entertainment' (in 'Irish Oral Tradition,' in *A View of the Irish Language*, ed. Brian Ó Cuív [Dublin, 1969], p. 55).
13. *A Literary History of Ireland* (London, 1899), p. 630.
14. To illustrate, Hyde quotes a verse the children were made to learn: 'I thank the goodness and the grace/Which on my birth have smiled,/

And made me in these Christian days/A happy English child!' He also quotes from one of the elementary books: ' "On the east of Ireland is England, where the Queen lives. Many people who live in Ireland were born in England, *and we speak the same language, and are called one nation"* ' (*Lit. Hist.*, p. 636; Hyde's italics).

15. For example William Larminie's *West Irish Folk Tales and Romances* (1893); Jeremiah Curtin's *Myths and Folk-lore of Ireland* (1890); *Hero-Tales of Ireland* (1894); and *Tales of the Faeries and of the Ghost World* (1895); and Lady Gregory's *Visions and Beliefs in the West of Ireland* (published 1920, but collected earlier). Lady Gregory's volume contains many stories from the Aran Islands, collected in 1898, the same year Synge first went there. Of her stories, Richard M. Dorson says 'they testified to the tenacious hold of the pre-Christian fairy faith upon the west-country folk' (*Folktales of Ireland* [Chicago, 1966], p. xx).

16. The Gaelic milieu does in some cases have so firm a hold in the culture that it survives even the death of the language. T. H. Mason shows this to be true of Inishmurray, an island off county Sligo, where 'distinctly pagan' traditions and customs persist. Mason says, 'One would imagine that with the loss of the native tongue the folklore and traditions would also disappear, but such is not the case on Inishmurray' (*The Islands of Ireland* [London, 1950], p. 27.

17. In reading about and discussing the quality of religious belief on the islands and Synge's ability to grasp it, I have found these issues clouded by defensiveness and bias. Roman Catholic commentators may wish to stress the regularity of the islanders' Christian beliefs and the inability of Synge – a defected Protestant – to understand them. Folklorists seem equally bent on maximizing the paganism of the culture and minimizing the Christian elements. I have tried to avoid the distorting effects of these points of view.

18. Daphne D. C. Pochin Mould, *The Aran Islands* (Newton Abbot, 1972), pp. 114-115. Nurse B. N. Hedderman wrote of her experiences on the islands in *Glimpses of My Life in Aran*. (Bristol, 1917).

19. According to P. A. Ó Síocháin, *Aran: Islands of Legend*, rev. ed. (Dublin, 1967), p. 183.

20. Seán Ó Súilleabháin, *Irish Wake Amusements* (Cork, 1967), p. 13. Translated by the author from the original Irish published in 1961.

21. Note the suggestion in the last-quoted passage that even the priests are perhaps not to be trusted to carry out the Church's strictures. Another case of *Hibernicis ipsis Hibernior*?

22. See Ó Súilleabháin, *Irish Wake Amusements*, chap. IX, esp. p. 137.

III

The Shock of Some Inconceivable Idea

i

David H. Greene reflects the consensus among Synge's critics when he says, 'Synge's visit to the Aran Islands in 1898 must be one of the most remarkable examples on record of how a sudden immersion in a new environment converted a man of ostensibly mediocre talent, a complete failure, in fact, into a writer of genius.' (Greene/Stephens, p. 74). Almost everyone agrees that the turning point in Synge's creative life was his going to the Aran Islands, supposedly at the prompting of W. B. Yeats in December of 1896.[1] Certainly the years leading up to Synge's first visit to the islands in May of 1898 were unproductive and must have been filled with difficulty and self-searching. He had been travelling between Dublin and various European cities for several years, he had given up the musical career that was his original reason for going to Germany in 1893, and he must have been admitting to himself that his true wish was to be a writer, not a Romance philologist or critic. He did not, however, have sufficient faith in his literary abilities to proclaim himself a writer. Though he had written drafts of poems and plays, he had published only one literary work – a mediocre sonnet in the Trinity College magazine in 1893.[2] This fact, and the poor quality of the literary material that survives from this period, make the change that came about all the more remarkable.[3] To this point – May of 1898 – Synge had written nothing of any literary merit, yet in the little more than a decade before he died, he wrote some of the finest plays in English since the Renaissance. Clearly something happened that enabled the expression of his genius, and most critics have seen the Aran Islands experience as crucial to it.[4]

Most commentators have given two specific answers to the question of what Synge found in the islands that transformed him into a writer. The first answer is that here he found the living

72

traditions of a folk literature, and he found stories and incidents that lent themselves to dramatic use. The second is that among these people whose English was colored by their native Gaelic, Synge found a living language, one capable of being made into a worthy literary vehicle. As David H. Greene put it, 'The people of Aran had provided him with the material and the idiom with which he could construct an art completely different from any he had even dreamed of.' (Greene/Stephens, p. 80). It is true that *conte* and language are significant, distinctive elements in Synge's work, and Synge has acknowledged his debt to the islands in these regards. But this is too simple an explanation for what happened. Though several of his plays grow out of Aran stories, Synge did not use any of the stories as he heard them; rather, he significantly adapted and modified them. Moreover, there is clear evidence that Synge's interest in the Anglo-Irish dialect long predated his going to the islands.

Edward Stephens points out that 'Side by side with this restricted language [of his family] he [John] knew from childhood the rich imaginative rhythmical dialect common to East Wicklow, and preserved among the people of the plateau and the hills, as safe from outside influence as if they lived on an island. He was familiar with it in all its phases, whether in current conversation with the country people, or in the wild curses of brawling tinkers fighting when he happened to pass, or in the blessing of some tramping woman, who begged a penny as he pushed his bicycle up a hill'. (Typescript, p. 346). Stephens goes on to point out that under the influence of Archbishop Richard Chenevix Trench's *English, Past and Present* (1855), John found a particular interest in the Wicklow language: 'This was a new light on the value of the curious local dialect to which he was accustomed, a dialect containing words borrowed from English provincial speech on the one hand, and gaelic [sic] on the other, and using a syntax that was partly English and partly Gaelic in origin. His family regarded it as the amusing speech of the uneducated classes, but John began to note with greater attention than before the force and meaning of the phrases he heard, when he was walking or cycling through the country.' (Typescript, p. 347). T. R. Henn is correct when he says that Synge's characters speak 'a selection, refraction, compression of the language that Synge had known from boyhood, among the people of the Dublin, Wicklow and Galway countryside. It is *reinforced* and *enriched* by his life in the Aran Islands and in West Kerry.'[5]

The chronology of Synge's development also suggests that his responding to the Aran Islands was a complex process. Synge's first visit to the islands was in the summer of 1898, and he returned for successive visits in the autumns of 1899, 1900, 1901, and 1902. But even though his first, longest, visit was in 1898, the artistic effects of the islands did not appear until some four years later, in 1902, after he had completed a version of his book, *The Aran Islands.* In that year, Synge wrote *Riders to the Sea* and *The Shadow of the Glen,* and he drafted *The Tinker's Wedding.* Robin Skelton calls 1902 Synge's *Annus mirabilis,* and asks why it was so extraordinarily creative a year for him. (*J. M. Synge and his World,* p. 70). Recasting that question may focus the present point: If the Aran Islands experience was so meaningful for Synge, if it did transform him from mediocre talent into first class writer, why did the process take so long? If all he lacked to be a writer were the relatively concrete elements of plot and language, and if he found these on the islands, why this long dormancy? The reason is that the experience on the islands influenced Synge deeply and complexly, and required a period of gestation before it could manifest itself in his creative writing. It required, it seems, his writing a draft of his book-length essay on the Aran Islands before the experiences were sufficiently assimilated that he could draw on them for the creation of drama.[6]

W. B. Yeats did suggest that the islands were more for Synge than a source of language and plots, and some critics have echoed and tentatively pursued his hints. Yeats suggested that the islands served as a kind of 'objective correlative', enabling Synge to find in their geography and their culture a means of objectifying his thoughts and feelings. As Yeats put it, 'He was a drifting silent man full of hidden passion, and loved wild islands, because there, set out in the light of day, he saw what lay hidden in himself.' ('J. M. Synge and the Ireland of his Time', in *Essays and Introductions,* p. 330). Ann Saddlemyer pursues this tack in her essay 'Art, Nature, and "The Prepared Personality",' where she argues that 'the adventures he records on the Aran Islands also reflect the contours, emotions and temperament of the author's personality, for this journey to the western world was also an exploration and revaluation of his own consciousness.'[7] Robin Skelton implies something similar when he describes *The Aran Islands* as involving 'a system of values alien to all his previous experience, and a perspective upon the nature of cultural inheritance'. (*The Writings of J. M. Synge,* p. 30). But for all these suggestions the impact of Synge's experiences on the islands has not been sufficiently related to his psychology and his background, nor have its effects in his plays been fully shown.

What Synge got from these islands was not simply plots and language; it was rather a way of looking at reality, and an appreciation of the vast if implicit role played by our received cultural and intellectual assumptions. Among these primitive people living on the verge of the Western world, Synge found an archaic, pre-logical world view, qualitatively different from what he had known before. This complex experience could not be quickly reaped and harvested; it required slow winnowing. Eventually it gave Synge the new awareness and the new perspective that opened to him a variety of dramatic subjects and devices.

ii

The Aran Islands is an indispensable index to what aspects of the islands' culture most attracted and influenced Synge. As such, it brings together the two elements discussed in preceding chapters: Synge's state of mind on going there, and the milieu of the islands. In this regard, the most striking and important feature of the book is how frequently he describes the people as 'primitive' or 'archaic' and how persistent is his interest in the primitive aspects of their life.[8] He speaks of these islands as 'these few acres at the extreme border of Europe', or as a 'little corner on the face of the world'.[9] Of Inishmaan he says point-blank that 'the life is perhaps the most primitive that is left in Europe' (p. 53), and he speaks of the 'primitive babble' (p. 79) of the people as they load their horses onto the hooker. When he says of their belief that a needle protects against the fairies, 'Iron is a common talisman with barbarians . . .' (p. 80), he suggests something prehistoric about them. Similar comments throughout the book make it clear that Synge did regard this life as primitive and archiac, and that he was fascinated by these aspects of it.[10]

This primitivism influenced Synge in two distinguishable ways. First, the archaic culture of the islands provided an alternative world view especially appropriate to Synge's own needs and wishes, one involving a free expression of emotion and a wholeness of reponse that seemed to him particularly enviable. As we shall see, Synge's use of the epithets *primitive* and *archaic* always connotes some unity or wholism in the people's experience, some ability to yield the ego to a larger reality. Second, it provided an opportunity to see and feel reality from a perspective different

from any he had ever known; it was a challenge to his mind and
to his emotions, and it enabled him to see the arbitrariness of
many of the ideas and attitudes he had always taken for granted.

Synge talks on several occasions about his attempts to
empathize with the people, or about how different in the most
implicit parts of their experience they are. He describes his
riding in a curagh as follows: 'It gave me a moment of exquisite
satisfaction to find myself moving away from civilization in this
rude canvas canoe of a model that has served primitive races
since men first went on the sea'. (p. 57). Of the people of Inishmaan he says, 'I cannot yet judge these strange primitive natures
closely enough to divine them. I feel only what they are.' (p. 102,
fn.). In his most extended statement of this sort he says,

> In some ways these men and women seem strangely far away
> from me. They have the same emotions that I have, and the
> animals have, yet I cannot talk to them when there is much to
> say, more than to the dog that whines beside me in a mountain
> fog.
> There is hardly an hour I am with them that I do not feel
> the shock of some inconceivable idea, and then again the shock
> of some vague emotion that is familiar to them and to me. On
> some days I feel this island as a perfect home and resting place;
> on other days I feel that I am a waif among the people. (p. 113).

We have already noted Synge's question to Yeats, 'Is not style
born out of the shock of new material?' This shock of new ideas
and new emotions was something Synge felt repeatedly on these
islands. In a fascinating notebook passage that did not get into
the printed text, Synge says:

> A heavy roll from the Atlantic is today on the north west of
> the island and the surf line is of wonderful splendour. I am used
> to it and look now backwards to the morning a few weeks ago
> when I looked out first unexpectedly over the higher cliffs of
> Aranmore, and stopped trembling with delight. A so sudden
> gust beautiful is a danger [sic]. It is well arranged that for the
> most part we do not realize the beauty of a new wonderful
> experience till it has grown familiar and so safe to us. If a man
> could be supposed to come with a fully educated perception of
> music, yet quite ignorant of it and hear for the first time let us
> say Lamoureux's Orchestra in a late symphony of Beethoven

I doubt his brain would ever recover from the shock. If a man could come with a full power of appreciation and stand for the first time before a woman – a woman perhaps who was very beautiful – what would he suffer? If a man grew up knowing nothing of death or decay and found suddenly a grey corpse in his path what would [he] suffer? Some such emotion was in me the day I looked first on these rising magnificent waves towering in dazzling white and green before the cliff; if I had not seen waves before I would have likely lost my sense. It would be an interesting if cruel experiment to bring some sensitive nature from the central portion of Ireland – who had never seen the sea – to carry him blindfold to Aran on a calm day and keeping [him] in confinement till a great storm arose lead him on the cliff and take away the cloth from his eyes. I am not able to imagine any shock more great. (pp. 97-98. Price prints this passage in a footnote, and says that it comes from Notebook 19).

Analogous shocks to Synge's own perceptions and world view made the Aran Islands experience uniquely valuable and fruitful to him.

Several passages in *The Aran Islands* suggest Synge's sense that the entire frame of mind among these people is so different from our own as to be almost untranslatable. An example is his repeated contention that ordinary concepts of the law are inapplicable to this culture:

This impulse to protect the criminal is universal in the west. It seems partly due to the association between justice and the hated English jurisdiction, but more directly to the primitive feeling of these people who are never criminals yet always capable of crime, that a man will not do wrong unless he is under the influence of a passion which is as irresponsible as a storm on the sea. If a man has killed his father, and is already sick and broken with remorse, they can see no reason why he should be dragged away and killed by the law. (p. 95).

* * *

Some time ago, before the introduction of police, all the people of the islands were as innocent as the people here remain to this day. I have heard that at that time the ruling proprietor and magistrate of the north island used to give any man who

had done wrong a letter to a jailer in Galway, and send him off
by himself to serve a term of imprisonment. (p. 95).

* * *

It seems absurd to apply the same laws to these people and
to the criminal classes of a city. The most intelligent man on
Inishmaan has often spoken to me of his contempt of the law,
and of the increase of crime the police have brought to
Aranmor. (p. 96).

* * *

The mere fact that it is impossible to get reliable evidence in
the island – not because the people are dishonest, but because
they think the claim of kinship more sacred than the claims of
abstract truth – turns the whole system of sworn evidence into
a demoralizing farce, and it is easy to believe that law dealings
on this false basis must lead to every sort of injustice. (p. 96).

Running through these statements is an implicit contrast between the concrete feelings and realities of the people's lives and
the abstract, procrustean law. The claim of kinship or of a compelling passion is tangible and emotive; that of the law is abstract
and theoretical and has no meaningful relationship to this society.
Here again we see Synge's sense of the potential tyranny of mere
theories, and of the possible disjunction between concept and
feeling.

Nowhere is this conflict between the two cultures more vividly
seen than in the eviction Synge describes:

At a sign from the sheriff the work of carrying out the beds
and utensils was begun in the middle of a crowd of natives who
looked on in absolute silence, broken only by the wild impreca-
tions of the woman of the house. She belonged to one of the
most primitive families on the island, and she shook with uncontrollable fury as she saw the strange armed men who spoke
a language she could not understand driving her from the
hearth she had brooded on for thirty years. For these people
the outrage to the hearth is the supreme catastrophe. They
live here in a world of grey, where there are wild rains and
mists every week in the year, and their warm chimney corners,
filled with children and young girls, grow into the consciousness

of each family in a way it is not easy to understand in more civilized places. (p. 89).

This passage is rich in implication. It shows again Synge's sense of the people's primitiveness and his interest in their strange emotions. It shows too his sense of distance between the two cultures, of the differences in their 'consciousness'. And, as in the passage about the law, it shows a conflict between an emotive reality and a theoretical, procrustean concept. The unity of this woman's life is destroyed by forces extraneous to her, economic and legal forces she cannot comprehend, represented by outsiders whom she cannot even understand. This is an example not simply of social injustice but of a conflict of worlds. Such statements leave little question that Synge regarded the people of these islands as primitive and as very different from those he was accustomed to move among in Dublin or Paris, and that he found here an opportunity to see things differently than he had seen them before.

iii

I suggested earlier that his describing the culture as primitive and archaic always connoted for Synge some harmony or wholism in the people's responses. With this in mind, I want to look at three specific facets of Synge's experiences: first, the face of nature that Synge saw on these islands, and the rapport with nature that he sensed among the people; second, the people's expression of strong, irrational emotions and their capacity for blending emotions that seem incongruous if not contradictory; third, the people's a-dogmatic attitude toward Christian belief and their tolerance for traditional Irish beliefs. Through these runs the common strand of some concrete, emotive reality being set against or threatened by some theoretical, conceptual formulation.

Synge had shown a strong interest in nature from his childhood, and we have seen that his mother shared his delight in the natural world and encouraged his study of it. His long trips into the Wicklow hills, his collections of birds' eggs and butterflies, his joining the Dublin Naturalists' Field Club, all testify to this. But the face of nature he saw on the Aran Islands was quite different from what he had seen in Wicklow. Day jaunts into the Wicklow hills can bring one into touch with a beautiful terrain that seems tolerant of, even sympathetic toward, man. In this soft, fecund setting, a Wordsworthian sense of nature as man's mentor and guardian comes easily.[11] And the excursion always ends with a return to a warm, solid hearth, where any eccentricity of the environment can soon be forgotten.

On the Aran Islands Synge found something radically different, for there the people lived in continual, unmitigated contact with the severest, most demanding aspects of nature. One of the key-notes of *The Aran Islands* is sounded on the opening page when Synge states simply: 'I have seen nothing so desolate'. (p. 49). Here Synge found rock, sea, and wind so severe and unrelenting that it is impossible for man to ignore nature or to regard it simply as benign; these people 'feel their isolation in the face of a universe that wars on them with wind and seas' (p. 75). As Synge took in the severity and barrenness of this world, his earlier, Wordsworthian sense of nature must have seemed naive indeed. Viewing this desolation, this unrelenting stone and sea, Synge must have felt that he was looking at a face of reality he had never before known. Synge found on these islands, especially on the smaller two, an almost complete absence of those ameni-ties of technology that cushion man's contact with nature.[12] There were no motorboats, no telegraph, and on the middle island no resident doctor or priest, not even a wheeled vehicle, and only one bit and saddle. (pp. 76, 79). The sea was both a source of susten-ance and their continual antagonist, and after the funeral of a young man whose drowned body was cast upon the shore, Synge thinks:

> I could not help feeling that I was talking with men who were under a judgment of death. I knew that every one of them would be drowned in the sea in a few years and battered naked on the rocks, or would die in his own cottage and be buried with another fearful scene in the graveyard I had come from. (p. 162).

Synge must have wondered whether the face of nature that these people saw was truer and more real than the softness and beauty of county Wicklow. The temptation in such a case is to regard the earlier, softer view as naive and childish, and to see the barrenness, severity, and antagonism of this environment as the truer view of reality. While Synge probably did entertain this attitude, it is doubtful that he capitulated to it. The island experi-ences did not make Synge simply substitute one view of reality for another, but rather made him aware of the incompleteness of any one perspective upon an infinitely complex reality. What the Aran people see in nature is true, but what Synge earlier found in Wicklow (and continued to find each summer) is true also.

For all the severity of the islands' environment, Synge was aware that the peoples' contact with nature did have its positive aspect, for they achieved a rapport with nature, a merging of the self with some larger power, that cosmopolitan people have long since lost and that Synge envied. In a notebook passage that was not included in the published text, Synge said 'I cannot say it too often, the supreme interest of the island lies in the strange concord that exists between the people and the impersonal limited but powerful impulses of the nature that is around them.' (p. 75, fn.). And another passage quoted by Price that did not get into the published text makes the same point: 'Their minds have been coloured by endless suggestions from the sea and sky, and seem to form a unity in which all kinds of emotion match one another like the leaves or petals of a flower. When this atmosphere of humanity is felt in the place where it has been evolved, one's whole being seems to be surrounded by a scheme of exquisitely arranged sensations that have no analogue except in some services of religion or in certain projects of art we owe to Wagner or Mallarmé.'[13] On Inishmaan especially Synge felt 'forced to believe in a sympathy between man and nature'. (p. 75). Later he says,

> Even after the people of the south island, these men of Inishmaan seemed to be moved by strange archaic sympathies with the world. Their mood accorded itself with wonderful fineness to the suggestions of the day, and their ancient Gaelic seemed so full of divine simplicity that I would have liked to turn the prow to the west and row with them for ever.
>
> I told them I was going back to Paris in a few days to sell my books and my bed, and that then I was coming back to grow as strong and simple as they were among the islands of the west. (p. 142).

This use of 'archaic sympathies' and 'divine simplicity' reveal the wholistic overtones these terms have for Synge, the assumption that primitive man had a more unified and harmonious experience than modern man. Other examples of this appear throughout *The Aran Islands*. In another context Synge said of the tinkers that they 'console us, one moment at least, for the manifold and beautiful life we have all missed who have been born in modern Europe'. (p. 199).

Several other passages similarly reflect the rapport of the people with the elements of nature, and I suspect that Synge so envied and emulated this state that he did to some degree achieve it. He claims for example to comprehend the language of the birds (p. 73), and, after describing a perilous trip from Inishmaan to Inishmor in a curagh, he says, 'I enjoyed the passage. Down in this shallow trough of canvas, that bent and trembled with the motion of the men, I had a far more intimate feeling of the glory and power of the waves than I have ever known in a steamer.' (p. 120). He also describes a night-experience on Inishmaan when he seemed for a time 'to exist merely in my perception of the waves and of the crying birds, and of the smell of seaweed' (p. 130), and he tells of a dream of ecstatic union which we will look at in detail later.

One interesting instance of the closer rapport of the island people with nature, and of their being 'pre-modern', appears in their attitude toward time and their ways of measuring it. While the people were interested in Synge's watch, and one asked to be given a clock, their minds were not adapted to clock-time. Synge says,

> While I am walking with Michael some one often comes to me to ask the time of day. Few of the people, however, are sufficiently used to modern time to understand in more than a vague way the convention of the hours, and when I tell them what o'clock it is by my watch they are not satisfied, and ask how long is left them before the twilight. (p. 66).

It is intriguing for us as it was for Synge to imagine a place where the 'convention of the hours' has so little hold on the people, or so little function or tangibility for them.

I turn now to the related motif in *The Aran Islands* concerning the people's displays of emotion, and the emotions that were induced in Synge himself. There are two aspects to Synge's interest in the people's emotions – first his fascination with strong emotions *per se,* as expressing a degree or mode of reality that is usually muted or disguised; second, his interest in emotions that seem 'incongruous' or 'illogical'. Several persons have noted Synge's fascination with strong emotion and have pointed to its recurrence in his works. Yeats said of Synge that he was 'a drifting silent man full of hidden passion, and loved wild islands, because there, set out in the light of day, he saw what lay hidden in himself. There is passage after passage where he dwells upon some moment of excitement.' ('J. M. Synge and the Ireland of his Time', in *Essays and Introductions*, p. 330). Synge's interest in incongruous emotion is shown continually in *The Aran Islands;* he several times remarks the strangeness of the people's response. This idea of incongruous emotion, explored earlier in regard to the wake, affords us another example of how feelings that seem so unquestionably natural or reasonable to one culture may be regarded quite differently in another. As we saw earlier, among our most implicitly held assumptions are those that certain emotions are inherently appropriate to certain experiences – that grief is natural to some occasions and laughter to others – and few experiences strike us more strangely than when our expectations about these emotions are not fulfilled. Yet Synge was frequently surprised by the emotional responses he found on these islands.

On several occasions Synge relates stories about displays of emotion that he found puzzling, disconcerting, or even frightening. One of these occurred when some pigs were being loaded onto the boat at Kilronan pier. Synge first notes the shrieking of the pigs, saying:

> . . . the animals shut their eyes and shrieked with almost human intonations, till the suggestion of the noise became so intense that the men and women who were merely looking on grew wild with excitement, and the pigs waiting their turn foamed at the mouth and tore each other with their teeth.

When the pigs were finally dispatched, amid tumult and screaming, Synge found himself left among the women and children, and with a strange remnant of the earlier excitation:

> The women were over-excited, and when I tried to talk to them they crowded round me and began jeering and shrieking at me because I am not married. A dozen screamed at a time, and so rapidly that I could not understand all they were saying, yet I was able to make out that they were taking advantage of the absence of their husbands to give me the full volume of their contempt. Some little boys who were listening threw themselves down, writhing with laughter among the seaweed, and the young girls grew red with embarrassment and stared down into the surf.

For a moment I was in confusion. I tried to speak to them,

but I could not make myself heard, so I sat down on the slip and drew out my wallet of photographs. In an instant I had the whole band clambering round me, in their ordinary mood. (pp. 137-38).

The emotion here is strange indeed, somewhat irrational, and Synge's consternation, bordering on fear, comes through clearly. We can feel, too, how relieved he is to find the device that breaks the developing emotions and returns the people to their 'ordinary mood'.

Synge also tells of a strange, perturbing laughter that he heard on Inishere.

While the curraghs were being put out I noticed in the crowd several men of the ragged, humorous type that was once thought to represent the real peasant of Ireland. Rain was now falling heavily, and as we looked out through the fog there was something nearly appalling in the shrieks of laughter kept up by one of these individuals, a man of extraordinary ugliness and wit.

At last he moved off towards the houses, wiping his eyes with the tail of his coat and moaning to himself 'Tá mé marbh' ('I'm killed'), till some one stopped him and he began again pouring out a medley of rude puns and jokes that meant more than they said.

There is quaint humour, and sometimes wild humour on the middle island, but never this half-sensual ecstasy of laughter. Perhaps a man must have a sense of intimate misery, not known there, before he can set himself to jeer and mock at the world. These strange men with receding foreheads, high cheek-bones, and ungovernable eyes seem to represent some old type found on these few acres at the extreme border of Europe, where it is only in wild jests and laughter that they can express their loneliness and desolation. (p. 140).

These two passages show how the strangeness of the island world coalesced itself for Synge around 'weird' emotions such as those described here. He describes the 'strange' men as if they were another species, not quite human, and we suspect that the laugher's 'extraordinary ugliness' is partly an objectification of Synge's fears. The phrase 'half sensual ecstasy of laughter' shows his fascination with the sound, but his inability to empathize with it.

Synge tells later of a quarrel between a man and a woman

that went on interminably and reached an appalling pitch. The account begins:

> About six o'clock I was going into the school-master's house, and I heard a fierce wrangle going on between a man and a woman near the cottages to the west, that lie below the road. While I was listening to them several women came down to listen also from behind the wall, and told me that the people who were fighting were near relations who lived side by side and often quarrelled about trifles, though they were as good friends as ever the next day. The voices sounded so enraged that I thought mischief would come of it, but the women laughed at the idea. Then a lull came, and I said that they seemed to have finished at last.
>
> 'Finished!' said one of the women; 'sure they haven't rightly begun. It's only playing they are yet.' (p. 152).

As Synge tells us, the argument went on for four hours, and though some spectators gathered, most people simply went on about their business, and Synge himself was drawn into playing his fiddle for a dance. Synge's lack of comprehension of the episode is shown by his false (though natural) fear that mischief would result, and by his presuming the quarrel done, while the women knew it was just begun. We are also surprised that the people could, after so terrible an eruption of emotion, be good friends the next day. This seems childlike, or primitive perhaps, rather than normal adult psychology. Synge tells also of a terrible knife fight that began in one man's teasing comment to the son of a good friend that he was sharpening his knife to kill the boy's father, and that quickly erupted into a violent fight in which five men died. But even stranger is the end of the story: ' "They buried them the day after, and when they were coming home, what did they see but the boy who began the work playing about with the son of the other man, and their two fathers down in their graves".' (p. 156).

In one brief section of Part IV, Synge gathers several incidents that are linked by the motif of pain and by the people's strange reaction to it:

> Although these people are kindly towards each other and to their children, they have no feeling for the sufferings of animals, and little sympathy for pain when the person who feels it is not in danger. I have sometimes seen a girl writhing and

howling with toothache while her mother sat at the other side of the fireplace pointing at her and laughing at her as if amused by the sight.

A few days ago, when we had been talking of the death of President M'Kinley [sic], I explained the American way of killing murderers, and a man asked me how long the man who killed the President would be dying.

'While you'd be snapping your fingers,' I said.

'Well,' said the man, 'they might as well hang him so, and not be bothering themselves with all them wires. A man who would kill a King or a President knows he has to die for it, and it's only giving him the thing he bargained for if he dies easy. It would be right he should be three weeks dying, and there'd be fewer of those things done in the world.'

If two dogs fight at the slip when we are waiting for the steamer, the men are delighted and do all they can to keep up the fury of the battle.

They tie down donkey's heads to their hoofs to keep them from straying, in a way that must cause horrible pain, and sometimes when I go into a cottage I find all the women of the place down on their knees plucking the feathers from live ducks and geese.

When the people are in pain themselves they make no attempt to hide or control their feelings. An old man who was ill in the winter took me out the other day to show me how far down the road they could hear him yelling 'the time he had a pain in his head.' (p. 163).

These passages show again Synge's interest in incongrous attitudes and responses, and in emotions that are too intense and compelling to be set aside by rational consideration or by social decorum.

I wish now to draw certain strands of *The Aran Islands* together by looking at a passage that wonderfully concentrates the themes we have been pursuing. We noted earlier Yeats's statement that Synge was attracted to these wild islands because he saw there 'what lay hidden in himself'. But even more important to him was the blend of man and nature he saw in these emotional states we have been considering. Synge found in these people a unity and intensity of emotion he felt to be simultaneously appealing and terrifying – appealing because of its concreteness and reality, terrifying because of the loss of self it involved. We have already looked at some of the emotions induced in Synge himself by this place and these people, but one further instance deserves special note. In a portion of *The Aran Islands* that was published separately in 1903 as 'A Dream on Inishmaan', Synge vividly describes a dream he had. The entire passage must be quoted:

Some dreams I have had in this cottage seem to give strength to the opinion that there is a psychic memory attached to certain neighbourhoods.

Last night, after walking in a dream among buildings with strangely intense light on them, I heard a faint rhythm of music beginning far away on some stringed instrument.

It came closer to me, gradually increasing in quickness and volume with an irresistibly definite progression. When it was quite near the sound began to move in my nerves and blood, and to urge me to dance with them.

I knew that if I yielded I would be carried away to some moment of terrible agony, so I struggled to remain quiet, holding my knees together with my hands.

The music increased continually, sounding like the strings of harps, tuned to a forgotten scale, and having a resonance as searching as the strings of the 'cello.

Then the luring excitement became more powerful than my will, and my limbs moved in spite of me.

In a moment I was swept away in a whirlwind of notes. My breath and my thoughts and every impulse of my body, became a form of the dance, till I could not distinguish between the instruments and the rhythm and my own person or consciousness.

For a while it seemed an excitement that was filled with joy, then it grew into an ecstasy where all existence was lost in a vortex of movement. I could not think there had ever been a life beyond the whirling òf the dance.

Then with a shock the ecstasy turned to an agony and rage. I struggled to free myself, but seemed only to increase the passion of the steps I moved to. When I shrieked I could only echo the notes of the rhythm.

At last with a moment of uncontrollable frenzy I broke back to consciousness and awoke.

I dragged myself trembling to the window of the cottage and looked out. The moon was glittering across the bay, and there was no sound anywhere on the island. (pp. 99-100).

Every aspect of this account has some interest for us. Synge's reference to a 'psychic memory attached to certain neighbourhoods' suggests that through his dream he was drawn into some supra-individual psychic entity (hardly a rationalist's notion!). The 'strange light' he refers to reminds us of other instances where qualities of light evoke distinctive emotional tonalities (see, for example, *CW,* II, 162). The 'faint rhythm of music' both confirms the value of Synge's musical experience as a vehicle into emotive experiences (see above, p. 35) and suggests Synge's use in other contexts of rhythm as enabling the individual to merge into some larger entity (see *CW,* II, 161-162).[14] But two points deserve special emphasis: the idea of the self-abandonment necessary to the ecstasy, of Synge's gradually and fearfully yielding himself to the emotive power of the music; and the ecstasy's turning to agony and rage upon reassertion of the self. The intensity, even ecstasy, of emotion expresses Synge's probably exaggerated sense of what unity and depth of feeling await us if we can get beyond conscious individuality, if we can yield ourselves to the greater powers and deeper rhythms of nature. But Synge's fearful reluctance and the ecstasy's turning to rage express Synge's deep suspicion and fear of yielding the integrity of his self. Whether such intense, ecstatic states do await us beyond the edge of individuality, few can say, but I suspect that these descriptions take a heightened coloring from the value this reserved, self-contained man read into them. To be forced, or to be *able,* to yield to an emotion so intense, so beyond rational consideration, seemed to Synge both appealing and terrifying.

The people of the Aran Islands have for centuries been Roman Catholic. But *The Aran Islands* shows that Synge found to be true what we have seen suggested by others – that Gaeltacht Irish are so undogmatic about matters of belief that they feel little compulsion to confine themselves to the orthodoxies of the church (see above, pp. 62-65). The old beliefs in the fairies, in the living dead, in miracles of various sorts, are shown continually. Nor do we get any great sense of clash or conflict between the pagan and the orthodox attitudes. On the contrary, there is a blending and an accommodation of them that is impressive and occasionally amusing, though it might not be so regarded by the bishop.

Synge's account is filled with evidence that the people still talk of, believe in, and experience the 'little people' of traditional Irish lore. Many of the traditional types of fairy stories are related, with no apparent sense of an incongruity between these and orthodoxy. We hear of a man's child being taken by the fairies (p. 51), of seed potatoes full of blood (p. 51), of a farmer who borrows flour from the fairies (pp. 80-82), of women who were 'away' with them (p. 80), of a storm raised by the power of a native witch (p. 88), of rye turned into oats (p. 127), of someone seeing a convention of the dead of the two smaller islands (p. 157), of the hosting of four or five hundred of the fairies on horses (p. 159), of a woman's seeing her dead son riding a horse (p. 164), of heel marks left by the fairies' playing ball in the night (p. 165), of ships that disappear (pp. 165, 181-82), and so on.

Though he made few explicit comments about it, Synge was perfectly aware of the strange climate of belief he was inhabiting. He says, for example, 'These people make no distinction between the natural and the supernatural' (p. 128), and he observes:

My intercourse with these people has made me realize that miracles must abound wherever the new conception of law is not understood. On these islands alone miracles enough happen every year to equip a divine emissary. Rye is turned into oats, storms are raised to keep evictors from the shore, cows that are isolated on lonely rocks bring forth calves, and other things of the same kind are common.

The wonder is a rare expected event, like the thunderstorm or the rainbow, except that it is a little rarer and a little more wonderful. (pp. 128-29).

Synge's unelaborated phrase 'the new conception of law' is interesting. By this he apparently refers to the law of science and rationalism, of physical cause and effect, that has permeated the western mind and has exorcized the sense of wonder. These people, he suggests, have not succumbed to this, and retain the sense of wonder and of the continual interplay of natural and supernatural that men more commonly had before the advent of scientific empiricism.

Synge's own orthodoxy-influenced perspective emerges in a comment he makes after hearing a mixture of keens and prayers for the dead at a funeral. He says, 'There was an irony in these words of atonement and Catholic belief spoken by voices that were still hoarse with the cries of pagan desperation.' (p. 75). This testifies to the blending of pagan and Christian, and to Synge's awareness of it. But the irony he feels arising out of a tension between these elements exists only in himself, not in the people.

This is one of several indications in *The Aran Islands* that orthodoxy and paganism coexist quite peacefully in the culture. Another is the Catholic theory of the fairies, given by Old

Mourteen, who explains that when God was casting out Lucifer and his cohorts, 'an archangel asked Him to spare some of them, and those that were falling are in the air still, and have power to wreck ships, and to work evil in the world'. (p. 56). When it comes to protecting themselves against the demons of the other world, the people may draw, indiscriminately, upon some folk belief or upon the power of the cross. Pat Dirane told Synge how to protect himself from the fairies: '"Take a sharp needle," he said, "and stick it in under the collar of your coat, and not one of them will be able to have power on you".' (p. 80). (Synge's comment on this is 'Iron is a common talisman with barbarians. . . .') Later, another man tells Synge about visitations from the fairies and another mode of protection:

'I heard some of the boys talking in the school a while ago,' he said, 'and they were saying that their brothers and another man went out fishing a morning, two weeks ago before the cock crew. When they were down near the Sandy Head they heard music near them, and it was the fairies were in it. I've heard of other things too. One time three men were out at night in a curagh, and they saw a big ship coming down on them. They were frightened at it, and they tried to get away, but it came on nearer them, till one of the men turned round and made the sign of the cross, and then they didn't see it any more.' (p. 165).

These accounts suggest an easy interplay indeed between pagan and Christian and illustrate Alfred Nutt's suggestion that 'in dealing with powers so capricious . . . the wise man accepts all the help he can get' (see above, p. 64).

Another story not only shows the blending of these strands but suggests that the people make a greater distinction between Catholic and Protestant than between pagan and Catholic:

'Another time,' he went on, 'I was coming down where there is a bit of a cliff and a little hole under it, and I heard a flute playing in the hole or beside it, and that was before the dawn began. Whatever anyone says there are strange things. There was one night thirty years ago a man came down to get my wife to go up to his wife, for she was in childbed.

'He was something to do with the lighthouse or the coastguards, one of them Protestants who don't believe in any of these things and do be making fun of us. Well, he asked me to go down and get a quart of spirits while my wife would be getting herself ready, and he said he would go down along with me if I was afraid.

'I said I was not afraid, and I went by myself.

'When I was coming back there was something on the path, and wasn't I a foolish fellow, I might have gone to one side or the other over the sand, but I went on straight till I was near it – till I was too near it – then I remembered that I had heard them saying none of those creatures can stand before you and you saying the *De Profundis*, so I began saying it, and the thing ran off over the sand and I got home.

'Some of the people used to say it was only an old jackass that was on the path before me, but I never heard tell of an old jackass would run away from a man and he saying the *De Profundis*.' (p. 180).

These examples and stories speak for themselves in illustrating the people's blend of orthodoxy and paganism, but two aspects deserve re-emphasis. First, the pervasive, almost unremarked, belief in varieties of supernatural experiences, experiences that by any modern, rational standards are simply unbelievable. Second, the people's lack of any sense of incongruity, much less guilt, in their continual blending of the orthodox and the pagan. For Synge's awareness of the first we have clear testimony, and his awareness of the second seems inevitable. We have already seen how seriously Synge took matters of belief, and how he had to pay for his own unorthodoxies with feelings of guilt and alienation, and in the loss of Cherrie Matheson. In this context he must have been forcibly struck by the difference between the guilt and anguish he suffered for his inability to believe in the doctrines of orthodox Protestant Christianity and the naive, guiltless ease with which these people blended Christianity and paganism. Why should concern about fidelity to belief have played so traumatic a part in his own life, and so trivial a part in theirs? If 'apostasy' was real enough to produce grief and guilt in him, how could these people be so immune to its effects? Synge must have dwelt upon these questions, and the result was to impel him toward a sense of how powerful and persuasive a role our implicit attitudes play in our lives, and yet how arbitrary, how culturally variable, these implicit attitudes are.

iv

In this selective foray into *The Aran Islands,* I have drawn attention to motifs and events reflecting Synge's reactions to the islands.[15] My point is that the island experience was valuable to Synge because it immersed him in a culture with perspectives and attitudes qualitatively different from those he had known in Dublin or Paris. While certain specific attitudes in that culture doubtless appealed to him – its holistic 'simplicity' – its main value was in making him aware of the cultural variability of deeply implicit attitudes and beliefs. It was this awareness, winnowed during 1898 to 1901 as he drafted *The Aran Islands,* that gave Synge the impetus to write and provided an important part of his subject matter. As we shall see in succeeding chapters, each of his plays reflects in some way Synge's concern with the power and variability of implicit ideas and attitudes. This may express itself as a dramatic shock given to his audience by eliciting and then undermining their implicit ideas; it may occur as an attempt to evoke in drama a cultural milieu incompatible with received Western modes of thought; it may occur as a dramatic confrontation between two cultures; it may occur as a deeper exploration of the philosophical implications, dark or bright, of the relations between ideas and reality; it may occur as Synge's own dedicated attempt to realize and evade his contemporaries' stereotyped attitudes towards dramatic material.

To what extent Synge's realizations relieved his guilt about divergence from his family's dogmas, or enabled him to hold more freely some of his own nascent beliefs, is difficult to say. Probably his insights did encourage him to hold more firmly to his beliefs about the reality of tone or mood, about the possibility of rapport between man and nature, and about the possibility of unifying thought and feeling in action. That they helped his relationship with his family seems doubtful. Certainly he could not tell his mother and brothers that he had learned how unabsolute Christian doctrine and Western logic are, or that he had come to see that their own doctrinal differences were insignificant and should be subordinated to family unity. Such relativism would have appalled them as much as downright atheism. Whether these realizations ameliorated Synge's own guilt about his unorthodoxy and his differences with his family, I cannot say. They should have, but there is always a gap between what we know in theory and what we can put into practice, and by this time his relationship with them was firmly fixed.

Again I would stress that the result of Synge's experiences was not to convert him to primitivism, but to sensitize him to aspects of both cultures. Clearly he stood between the two, often sympathizing with, even envying, aspects of the islanders' experience, but never simply becoming one of them. This is evident in his statement that 'I can feel more with them than they can feel with me, and while I wander among them, they like me sometimes, and laugh at me sometimes, yet never know what I am doing'. (p. 113). This inevitable distance expresses itself too in his comparison of an island girl with a Raphael figure, and his viewing the folk stories of the islands through comparative mythology (see pp. 54, 57, 65). Ann Saddlemyer is quite right when she says, 'Standing between this primitive world and the artificial, civilized life which has trained him, Synge can sympathize with and sometimes share, but he can never belong to Aran.'[16] It was in fact his standing between two cultures that fertilized his mind and imagination and propelled him into writing of his plays.

NOTES TO CHAPTER III

1. Exactly when Yeats gave Synge this advice remains uncertain, but it seems unlikely that it was as early as December 1896. They first met on December 21, 1896, for Synge's diary for that day says 'Fait la connaissance de W. B. Yeates', and there are subsequent references to several meetings with Yeats and with Maud Gonne. In his Preface to *The Well of the Saints,* which was dated January 27, 1905, Yeats refers to his having first met Synge and given him the advice 'six years ago' in Paris, which would have been in 1899, well after Synge's first visit to the islands. But Yeats later thought better of this and wrote to Lady Gregory in 1911, 'Tell Bourgeois that I met Synge in Paris long before he had ever been in Aran. I met him in 1896, and our conversation about his going to Aran was published in the introduction to the first edition of *Well of the Saints* during Synge's lifetime' (quoted in Greene/ Stephens, p. 74). In that Preface Yeats tells us, 'I said: "Give up Paris. You will never create anything by reading Racine, and Arthur Symons will always be a better critic of French literature. Go to the Aran Islands. Live there as if you were one of the people themselves; express a life that has never found expression." I had just come from Aran, and my imagination was full of those grey islands where men must reap with knives because of the stones'. (*Essays and Introductions,* p. 299). This statement, if accurate, would date the conversation in 1896, for

Yeats's journey had taken place in the summer of 1896. But there is evidence that Yeats indeed did not see things so clearly at this juncture, and that he continued for some time to think of Synge as a potential critic of French literature. This would render Yeats's whole account doubtful, for as he presents it, his advice to go to the islands was a part of a call for Synge to turn away from French criticism. Edward Stephens was clearly of the opinion that Yeats thought of Synge as a critic long after 1896, and he cites evidence for this in his Typescript biography. He describes a meeting between Yeats and Synge in November of 1897, saying 'He [Synge] told Yeats that he had been planning a return to Paris in order to continue his study of literary criticism. Yeats did not, at that time, see into the future clearly enough to advise him to work in Ireland, but approved John's plan for going back to Paris'. (Typescript, p. 929). Stephens also quotes from a letter of Mrs Synge to Robert on December 10, 1897, saying 'He [Synge] has been very anxious to go away to Paris. He had been advised by his friend Yeats, the Irish poet, to go in for reviewing French literature so John is working away with that end in view'. (Typescript, p. 931). Stephens also calls attention to the undated letter from Yeats to Lady Gregory which she prints in *Our Irish Theatre* (p. 121), saying 'He [Synge] is really a most excellent man. He lives in a little room which he has furnished himself; he is his own servant. He works very hard and is learning Breton; he will be a useful scholar.' Whatever the date of this letter, it shows that Yeats did not on his first meeting advise Synge to turn away from criticism. And Stephens says in the Typescript that the context of the letter suggests that it was written not in 1896, but in 1899. (Stephens' basis for the 1899 date is not fully clear; perhaps it is that Synge did not furnish his own rooms in Paris until November of 1898.)

2. The sonnet 'Glencullen' appeared in the Hilary Term, 1893, issue of *Kottabos*. It is printed in R. Skelton's edition of the *Poems* (Oxford, 1962), p. 3.

3. This material consists in large part of poems written from 1892 onwards. Robin Skelton prints some of it in his edition of the *Poems*, but Synge's Notebooks contain many other examples of mediocre verse that Skelton neither publishes nor describes. Many of the poems are so poor that no one could have detected literary ability in the man who wrote them.

4. One exception is Donna Gerstenberger who contends that Synge had 'undergone most of the significant formative experiences of his life' before his first visit to the islands and says 'it is most doubtful, therefore, that the journeys to Aran gave Synge either his attitude toward life or his major themes'. (*John Millington Synge* [New York, 1964], p. 16).

5. *The Plays and Poems of J. M. Synge* (London, 1968), p. 11. My italics.

6. Synge kept notebooks during each of his visits to the islands, and he published an essay reflecting his island experience as early as November 1898. He also had a draft of his book-length essay far enough along by the summer of 1901 that Lady Gregory and Yeats read it, and he submitted the manuscript to Grant Richards for consideration in November of 1901. Although he did some revisionary work later, he had largely completed the book before he wrote his plays. Alan Price quotes from a letter Synge wrote to Spencer Brodney in December of

1907: 'I look on *The Aran Islands* as my first serious piece of work – it was written before any of my plays.' (*Coll. Works*, II, 47).

7. Saddlemyer's essay is in S. B. Bushrui, *Sunshine and the Moon's Delight* (1972), pp. 107-20. The quoted passage is on p. 107. A more recent essay by Saddlemyer – seen by me after the present manuscript was accepted for publication – offers a perceptive discussion of Synge's philosophy and his spiritual values, in ways congruent with arguments I propose in this essay. See 'Synge and the Doors of Perception' in Andrew Carpenter, ed., *Place, Personality and the Irish Writer* (1977), pp. 97-120.

8. Synge's interest in the primitive features of the life is obvious and has been noted or discussed by a number of critics, including Maurice Bourgeois, Herbert Frenzel, Robin Skelton, and Ann Saddlemyer.

9. The text of *The Aran Islands* is that in the Oxford *Collected Works*, Vol. II, edited by Alan Price (1966). These passages occur on pp. 140 and 162. Future annotations are given parenthetically in the text.

10. For other uses of 'primitive' or 'prehistoric' or 'archaic' in describing the people, see *Coll. Works*, II, 47, 57, 89 (twice), 102 fn., 114, 132, 134, 142, 178. There are analogous statements about Irish myth and literature in several of Synge's essays and reviews; see *Coll. Works* II, 354, 365, 368, 370, 375.

11. Wordsworth was for several years Synge's favorite poet. Cherrie Matheson's statement that Synge told her he 'preferred Wordsworth to any other English poet' seems reliable, for it is supported by Edward M. Stephens, and much of Synge's early verse was clearly Wordsworthian. Cherrie says 'he [Synge] said he [Wordsworth] was more at one with Nature.' Yeats comments that such a phrase 'is too vague to increase our knowledge, but it recalls some early work of Synge's, certain boyish reveries. . . .' (*Irish Statesman*, July 5, 1924, p. 532).

12. In a footnote to the preceding chapter I noted Synge's preference for the smaller islands. He spent most of his time on the middle island, Inishmaan, which he found the most primitive. The largest island, Inishmor, seemed to Synge too close to a replica of life on the mainland. He says, 'Compared with them [Inishere and Inishmaan] the falling off that has come with the increased prosperity of this island [Inishmor] is full of discouragement. The charm which the people over there share with the birds and flowers has been replaced here by the anxiety of men who are eager for gain. The eyes and expression are different, though the faces are the same, and even the children here seem to have an indefinable modern quality that is absent from the men of Inishmaan' (p. 116). His few comments comparing Inishere and Inishmaan show that, in social structure at least, he regarded the south island as 'more advanced' (i.e. more modern) than the middle one (p. 140).

13. *CW*, II, 102 fn. (Price cites p. 87 of the Typescript in Box-file G). For other comments on the people's rapport with nature, see *CW*, II, 59, 66, 74, 114, 139 and 143 fn.

14. The role of rhythm in the works and theories of Yeats, Synge, and A. E. deserves study. All three seem to regard rhythms as crucial in enticing appropriate emotions to incarnate themselves into literary works.

15. My account does not claim to meet scholars' need for a full and satisfying discussion of the nature and the structure of *The Aran Islands*. Several critics have suggested that the work – whether we call it

documentary, memoir, essay – has an admirable unity, but no one has done justice to this idea. For a review of relevant discussions, see pp. 356-359 of my chapter on Synge in *Anglo-Irish Literature: A Review of Research* (New York, 1976). The only subsequent discussion is Malcolm Kelsall's 'Synge in Aran', *Irish University Review,* V, 2 (Autumn 1975), 254-270. Kelsall's interest is more in Synge's temperament than in the structure of *The Aran Islands.* He contends that Synge's aestheticism and morbidity prevented his seeing the 'Homeric' qualities in island life. Kelsall says of *The Aran Islands,* 'Probably he [Synge] was unaware that he was composing a work of fiction' (p. 254).

16. In 'Art, Nature, and "The Prepared Personality",' in S. B. Bushrui, *Sunshine and the Moon's Delight* (Gerrards Cross and Beirut, 1972), p. 114.

IV

First Fruits: *The Shadow of the Glen;*
Riders to the Sea; The Tinker's Wedding

i

We turn now to Synge's six plays. My discussions of the plays
are not designed primarily to provide new interpretations. Rather,
the aim and the approach will vary from play to play, in order to
highlight whatever is most important in terms of the ideas we are
pursuing. When the point I am making involves the significance
of audience reaction or the claim that Synge intended to frustrate
stereotyped response, then attention must be given to audience
response or critical reception. When interest lies more specifically
in the themes of the play, the approach becomes more analytical.

This aim is admittedly limited, but it is nevertheless significant.
It is important first of all in that it offers an opportunity to see
how an individual artistic mind and its milieu interact to result in
literary themes and dramatic devices. It is significant too because
the strand being pursued pervades Synge's works: it appears as
theme, as situation, as dramatic device, as authorial attitude. I
shall resist calling it the single most important feature of the
plays, but I do believe it to lie very close to the heart of Synge's
concerns as a dramatist and as a man. And the strand we are
pursuing is comprehensive and persistent enough to reveal a
pattern of development that runs through all six plays.

The underlying claim is that the mind-shaking experiences
Synge had on the Aran Islands manifest themselves in a variety
of themes and devices in his plays. One dramatic result of Synge's
coming to appreciate the power of our received assumptions or
stereotypes is his penchant for evoking predictable political or
religious reactions from his audience, and then undercutting those
reactions. That *The Shadow of the Glen* was denounced, *The
Playboy of the Western World* rioted, and *The Tinker's Wedding*

denied staging is no accident. A part of Synge's aim in these plays was to put his audience through an experience of shock, of cognitive dissonance, similar to what he suffered upon reading Darwin, or to what he enjoyed on the Aran Islands. Closely related to this is Synge's wish to evade those generic stereotypes such as comedy or tragedy, representing as they do received Western categories of response. His aim was to do justice to the complexity, perhaps even the incongruity or irrationality, of his characters' feelings or their milieu, without regard for whether the result fell into a recognizable genre. He would, I believe, have been amused by how much critical energy has been spent in attempting to pigeon-hole his plays and would have seen this as another expression of the need to vindicate received ideas, for some critics have been more concerned to label the plays than to understand them. The fact that several of the plays turn on confrontations between persons expressing radically different world views also stems from the insights Synge gained by standing between two cultures on the Aran Islands, and his fascination with strong emotions in his characters reflects the power and reality he found in such emotions among the islanders. Beneath the surface of the plays, one of Synge's most persistent themes involves the relationship between our abstractions and the "reality" we see through them. Implicit to some degree in all of the plays, this theme is present whenever a character projects a dream or comes to realize the falsity of ideals he has been pursuing. This theme receives its fullest exploration in *The Well of the Saints* and *The Playboy of the Western World,* where Synge dramatizes the results of his realizing that our ideas and ideals are to a great extent socially derived and arbitrary. He pursues the question of whether ideas have any meaningful relation to 'reality', of why some of our abstractions are 'lies' and others are 'dreams' – why some betray us and others challenge or fulfill us. And in exploring this issue of the relation between abstractions and reality, Synge suggests that language has unique power as the medium by which mind and reality are able to interpenetrate.

There is even a complementary and progressive pattern in these concerns as we move from play to play. Not that there was any program of this sort in Synge's mind; he was not sufficiently aware of these themes for that to be the case. But we can in retrospect see a pattern of development, and it forms the basis of the organization of my chapters discussing the plays. In this pattern, the first three plays present various restricted, specific aspects of these themes; *The Well of the Saints* and *The Playboy*

of the Western World represent larger-scale and more philosophical presentations of these implicit issues; and *Deirdre* shows
Synge using what he has learned to achieve a unique conception
of traditional dramatic material.

ii

The Shadow of the Glen, Synge's first successful play, involves
several devices and themes relevant to this study. The reception
of the play is itself germane to my point, for this is one of the
several of Synge's plays that evoked strong reaction from the
audience, and the critics who have written about it have often
fallen into the trap of approaching the drama through inappropriate categories or expectations. The original reviewers called
the play anti-Irish and immoral; Daniel Corkery charged it with
flaws of psychology and mood; and even such an admirer of
Synge as T. R. Henn has felt constrained to say of the apparent
twist at the play's ending, 'I do not find this scene incredible.'[1]
And David II. Greene has suggested that the ending swings the
play 'from its logical and sombre conclusion into the realm of
romantic symbolism', and that the 'spectator of the action must
also shift his ground from realism to symbolism.'[2] But while such
comments testify to the puzzlement many feel at the play's ending, these strictures reflect predispositions in the critics rather
than flaws in the drama; neither the concluding scene, nor the
psychology, nor any other facet of the play requires apology or
the invocation of 'symbolism'. If we can accept the play on its
own terms rather than demanding that it fulfil certain preconceptions, we shall find the psychology and mood quite harmonious
and the ending easily acceptable, even predictable.

This is not to say that Synge expected or wished us to see the
true lineaments of the play at first glance, or that all of these
critical strictures are smoke where there is no fire. The play is
potentially confusing, and is likely to leave its audience initially
puzzled or frustrated. Synge warned Frank Fay that this play
demanded 'an intellectual effort to make [it] comprehensible, or
at least a repeated hearing'.[3] But the temporary confusion is not
the result of a flaw in Synge's art; it is, rather, a part of his
aesthetic purpose, and is a recurrent feature of his drama. As we
shall see, most of Synge's plays have created problems for the
audience or the critics, ranging from consternation about the
genre the play belongs to, or puzzlement over how to respond to

a central character, to an outrage that expressed itself in riots. Several persons have remarked Synge's apparent wish to shock his audience, and there is some basis for the charge. *The Shadow of the Glen* did produce severe denunciation from several quarters, as well as a walkout by part of the acting company, and, later, some members of the audience; *Playboy* resulted in riots in Dublin and in the U.S.; Synge's draft of *A Play of '98* was squelched and *The Tinker's Wedding* refused production because it was feared they would produce trouble; and Robin Skelton even contends that Synge's early play *When the Moon Has Set* would have caused a riot.[4]

In *The Shadow of the Glen* as elsewhere in his works, Synge uses the artistic stratagem of throwing the viewer into confusion by evoking some traditional aesthetic stereotype, seeming to develop the play in terms of it, but then shifting the perspective so that the stereotype is frustrated. The result is an aesthetic shock or 'cognitive dissonance' which can be pleasing to the viewer if he open-mindedly goes on to carry the process through, see the stereotype shattered, and enjoy the author's skill in his stratagem as the true nature of the characters and events emerge. But if the audience has a vested interest in the stereotype and persists in maintaining it, the experience can be frustrating or angering. Part of Synge's purpose in *The Shadow of the Glen* was to produce this aesthetic shock of eliciting the traditional stereo-type of the lovers' triangle – the dissatisfied young wife, the jealous older husband, the young rival – and then shattering the stereotype by allowing the true natures and affinities of the characters to emerge at the end. The early attacks on the play, even Corkery's criticisms of it, are the effects of Synge's having succeeded quite well.[5]

There is little question that this play does cause initial con-fusion. For example, Padraic Colum, describing the first perform-ance of the play in Molesworth Hall in October, 1903, says, 'When the curtain fell on "The Shadow of the Glen" it was plain that the audience was disconcerted.'[6] This confusion arises from the audience's inclination to read into the play a pattern very common in Western literature. So strong is this tendency that they see in the play what they expect to see, and find it difficult to relinquish that expectation. This response involves an aesthetic form of what psychologists call 'perceptual set' – i.e. the set, or expectation, implicit in our perceptions of supposedly familiar things, our strong tendency to see what we expect to see.[7] And in this play, because the pattern of the traditional triangle gets firmly set in the mind, one typical reaction is puzzlement at the final scene, in which the husband and the young lover sit down together for a drink, since this baffles the usual understanding of the relationship between a husband and his rival.

This inclination to vindicate the stereotype has produced some amusing results. I have seen a staging of *The Shadow of the Glen* in which the final scene was played with Dan still pursuing Michael around the table, stick in hand, glowering at him. The words they spoke were, incongruously, those words of reconciliation written into the script, but the men were clearly antagonists, and they did not sit down together as the dialogue says they should. Apparently the director found the play as written inconsistent with his sense of what was going on, and he 'corrected' it.[8]

One of the contemporary reviews of the play provided a similar response. The reviewer in the *Irish Times* called the play 'excessively distasteful', and went on:

A mean and odious old man 'lettin' on to be dead' in bed while his pretty young wife provides refreshments for stray tramps, and is asked to arrange an immediate marriage with *a young suitor with whom she absconds* when her husband comes to life, seems to us an extraordinary choice of subject for a society that claims to have a higher and purer standard than ordinarily accepted in things dramatic. Mr. Synge has distinct power, both in irony and in dialogue, but surely he could display them better in showing in some other way – the way that should above all cast no slur on Irish womanhood – the wrong of mercenary marriage.[9]

The reviewer mis-summarized the play, saying that Nora leaves with her 'young suitor'. He did so, I believe, because of the strong pressure of the 'lovers' triangle' stereotype in his mind, causing him to see, or at least to remember, not what happened, but what he thought was going to happen.[10]

The early reviewers and critics denounced the play for its infidelity to Irish life and its slur upon Irish womanhood. But I suggest that these attacks and criticisms stemmed in large part not from moral outrage, but from aesthetic shock. The critic's frustration seeks for something to justify itself, and more often than not, this is some accusation of immorality or lack of patriotic feeling. Typical of the early reviews was Arthur Griffith's attack in his chauvinistic newspaper *The United Irishman*. Griffith, obviously offended by the play, stoutly denied any Irish quality to it. He said it was no more Irish than the *Decameron,* and he described it as a staging of a 'corrupt' version of that old-world libel on womankind, the Widow of Ephesus. He said that Synge was as 'utterly a stranger to the Irish character as any Englishman who has yet dissected us for the enlightenment of his countrymen'. Two weeks later Griffith again affirmed that the widow in Synge's play was the widow of Ephesus, *not* an Irish woman, and that Irish women were the most virtuous in the world.[11] Other contemporary reactions were as strangely based, if not so vituperative, and also charged the play with immorality or political perfidy.

Of such reactions Denis Johnston says, 'The arguments advanced against the play were sufficiently farfetched to confirm the suspicion that the real objections lay deeper in the psychology of the play's opponents.'[12] Some light can be cast on the workings of this psychology by another writer who shares some of Synge's thematic concerns. D. H. Lawrence, in his essay, 'Art and Morality', points out that Cezanne's still-lifes were reacted to as if they were somehow 'subtly immoral', somehow an attack on bourgeois morality, and that they inspired anger, hostility, and derisive resentment. Why, Lawrence asks, should a water pitcher and six apples inspire anger and resentment, and he answers: because they frightened the viewer by calling into question some of his most cherished notions about what the world out there is like. The paintings offended and frightened because they subtly challenged received attitudes, because instead of reinforcing stereotypes, as bad art often does, they challenged them and required that they be rethought.[13] This is precisely what *Shadow of the Glen* did. As Ann Saddlemyer has said, 'the audience, trained on traditional melodrama at the Queen's Theatre and led to expect another "Celtic" play in the Yeatsian tradition, were hardly prepared for *the shock of reality* to which Synge subjected them.'[14] Griffith's demand that the play meet his chauvinistic requirements, that it reinforce his image of Irish womanhood, and his denunciations when it failed to do so, are essentially analogous to what Lawrence has described.[15]

If Daniel Corkery's criticisms are less morally charged, they bear as clearly as Griffith's the marks of the frustration of his aesthetic expectations. Corkery begins his discussion by treating the play as if it were nothing other than a retelling of the familiar folktale. He says, 'The theme is as old as the hills: an old husband, a young wife; and Synge came by the story in the Aran Islands; but there is no peasant community in the world where it is not to be found.' (Corkery, p. 123). As Corkery goes on to talk at some length about the 'traditional story', it becomes clear that he approaches the play not on its own terms, but as another version of a received tale. In the wake of this he raises a question of generic integrity which others will subsequently raise about several of Synge's plays – he attacks it for wavering between comedy and tragedy: 'What is likely to happen then if the playwright, one truly under the spell of the folk mind, cannot rightly settle for himself whether his play, based on such a story, is to be comedy or tragedy? . . . Synge introduced so many elements that were contrary to the spirit of the comedy that one scarcely knows whether to call his play tragic or comic. Neither did Synge himself; neither does the audience.' (Corkery, p. 124). And Corkery comes back twice more to this question of whether the play is tragedy or comedy (pp. 125, 128). He goes on to criticize the psychology of the play as uncertain, and specifically refers to Nora Burke's character as 'disparate' (p. 126). He then says, 'The outstanding weakness of the play, however, is the aforesaid too rapid transitions from mood to mood that occur in it, no single mood being given the chance thoroughly to infect the mind with its own colour' (p. 128). Similarly, he says, 'The play is too small for such changes of mood as occur in it; and to use a musical term, there are no bridges between mood and mood' (p. 126). The problem of course is that Corkery is trying to fit the play, thematically and tonally, into a framework that Synge admittedly evokes, but that he never intended the play to fulfill. It is not that the psychology and mood are inconsistent, but that Corkery has been drawn into looking at them from a perspective that prevents his seeing them properly.

Both Griffith's and Corkery's criticisms of the play are, in their different ways, examples of what happens when a critic's expectations are frustrated. Griffith's is a barely articulate moral and political outrage, a flailing around for some justification for his dislike. Corkery's criticisms are more concrete and more subtle, but they are traceable to the same springs. His objection to the generic ambiguity of the play – is it to be tragedy or comedy? – reflects his frustrated wish to fit the play into some category and his inability to do so. As we shall see, this problem of generic categorization is persistent in criticism of Synge's plays. It arises from the critic's assumption that a drama must fulfill one or another of the received Western literary types, and Synge's unwillingness to have his plays do so. Corkery's objections to the psychology and mood of the play arise from his inability to fit

the characters, the events, and the tonal elements of the play into
patterns he presumes they should fulfill. But if we can see Nora
for what she is, her character is perfectly consistent from first to
last; she even represents a recurrent type among Synge's characters. Similarly, the changes in mood in the play flow naturally
from the nature of the characters and their changing relationships. They seem abrupt to Corkery only because he comes to
them with an expectation, a perceptual set, they were never
intended to fulfill.

With these suggestions in mind, let us look briefly at the
psychology within the play. For our purpose, the central character
is Nora, since she not only undergoes the greatest *apparent* change
of motivation, but also because Synge dramatizes in Nora the
necessity of being able to shift one's perspectives. She does this
both by being able to call her milieu into question and by her
ability to abjure her false image of Michael in time to save herself from life with him. But we must also look at Michael, the
would-be lover who ends up as drinking companion of the
husband.

The fact is that neither Nora nor Michael undergoes any
reversal of character during the play, only a clarification, and we
fail to see this immediately only because of the perspective
through which Synge brings us into the action. From the beginning Nora is pictured as discontented with the sedentary life of
the farm. She repeatedly complains of being lonesome, which in
Synge's terms means not that she lacks company, but that she
feels out of touch with life, feels that life is happening somewhere
else and is passing her by. When Michael comes in, we are anticipating him as her lover and the rival of the husband. But from
the point of Michael's entry, Synge offers suggestions that he is
not the man Nora needs or wishes him to be. We might suppose
that Nora finds in her young lover the vitality and respite from
loneliness she has not found with her old husband. But if we read
the signs carefully, we see that Michael is not a very good
example of the lover, and that Nora has to overlook some traits
and fabricate others to find in him an image adequate to her
needs. (The situation has clear analogies with *Playboy of the
Western World:* Michael is a Shawn Keogh whom Pegeen-Nora
is trying to see as a Christy.) What the strong-willed Nora wants
is a man who will give her life vitality and spirit, and in the
absence of anything better (Patch Darcy being dead), she turns to
Michael.

Their conversation about the mountain ewes clearly suggests

that Nora will have to look beyond Michael to find what she wants, and hints broadly of her greater kinship with the wandering tramps. Michael says 'Mountain ewes is a queer breed, Nora Burke, and I'm not used to them at all,' to which Nora replies, 'There's no one can drive a mountain ewe but the men do be reared in the Glen Malure, I've heard them say, and above by Rathvanna, and the Glen Imaal, men the like of Patch Darcy, God spare his soul, who would walk through five hundred sheep and miss one of them, and he not reckoning them at all.' Michael responds uneasily, 'Is it the man went queer in his head the year that's gone?' and Nora replies, 'It is surely,' to which the tramp adds, 'That was a great man, young fellow, a great man I'm telling you.'[16] No very subtle reading is required to foresee that Nora the mountain ewe will prove too much for timorous Michael to handle.

The true lines of kinship among the characters emerge when we hear Michael talk interestedly about the farm and money Dan has left behind, while Nora continues to disparage the fixed existence of even a good farm as lacking the life she needs. The old tramp feigns sleep during most of this conversation, but we learn later that he has followed it with interest.

The husband Dan's resurrection precipitates the situation and causes the characters to show their colours. Michael, in true Shawn Keogh fashion, turns to Nora for help, crying, 'Get me out of it, Nora, for the love of God' (*Coll. Works,* III, 53), and a few moments later, in response to her look of appeal, he says timidly, 'There's a fine Union [i.e. workhouse] below in Rathdrum.' (*Coll. Works,* III, 55). The tramp, who by now has seen the lay of the land and rises to Nora's defense, gives the erstwhile lover one more chance. When Dan turns Nora out, the tramp says of Michael, 'Maybe himself would take her,' but Michael says nothing and Nora says, 'What would he do with me now?' The affinity of Nora and the tramp becomes clear when he describes the life of the roads to her and she says, 'You've a fine bit of talk, stranger, and its with yourself I'll go.' (*Coll. Works,* III, 57). Their departure together is a consistent expression of their underlying similarities. Michael and Dan, now no longer separated by the superficial differences of husband and lover, show that they are brothers under the skin. They reveal their pragmatic, sedentary allegiance by sitting down to a drink together, toasting one another's good health and quiet life.

Looked at from this perspective, the psychology of the play is quite consistent, even straightforward. The characters emerge in two main types, common in Synge's works and in Anglo-Irish literature generally – the sedentary, practical, safe characters on the one hand, and the itinerant, imaginative, venturesome ones on the other. From the beginning the true affinities were between Dan and Michael, and between Nora and the tramp. It may take us some time to see that, but it is not very complex, much less contradictory. If we are willing to let the play speak for itself, willing to let it be what it is, not what we think it should be, we find in it not political defection or psychological inconsistency, but artistic subtlety and total harmony.

Another aspect of the play deserves discussion, since it provides further evidence of Synge's wish to call stereotypes into question. In his attacks on the play as un-Irish, Arthur Griffith contended that the play's source was 'a corrupt version of that old-world libel on womankind – the "Widow of Ephesus . . ." (Greene/Stephens, p. 148). Synge quickly denied this and pointed to a story he had been told on the Aran Islands as the source. There has been some subsequent discussion of this, but it seems clear now that the story Synge heard on the islands was the play's source, whatever analogues other literatures of the world may offer.[17]

Since this is the case, the changes Synge made as he rewrote the story into drama are interesting and relevant to our point. The story Synge heard from Pat Dirane is, as Daniel Corkery saw, a clear example of the stereotype we have referred to – the lovers' triangle of the older husband and the younger wife and lover. In it the suspicious old man feigns death to catch his younger wife with her lover. When the tramp comes in (Pat himself in his story), the husband reveals his plan and solicits help. The young wife and her lover come in and then retire into the bedroom. The story ends dramatically and predictably:

> Then the dead man got up, and he took one stick, and he gave the other to myself. We went in and saw them lying together with her head on his arm.
> The dead man hit him a blow with the stick so that the blood out of him leapt up and hit the gallery.
> That is my story. (*Coll. Works,* II, 70-72).

Earlier I noted that Synge's debt to the Aran Islands has been said to lie largely in the stories he heard there, and I pointed out that this is qualified by his adapting those stories. Here is an important example of such adaptation. The story Synge heard is a typical and complete fulfillment of the stereotype; the story he gives us in the play is radically different in that it elicits that stereotype, but then diverges drastically from it to produce an effect which is an integral part of his purpose in the play.

One other point deserves notice. To say that aesthetic shock and the frustration of a stereotype are purposes of this play still leaves a great deal unsaid. Aesthetic shock can be derived from the manipulation of any traditional material, and is in that sense a general aim. The particular material Synge chose for manipulation reflects more specifically his recurrent interests and themes. As Alan Price points out, *The Shadow of the Glen* is typical of Synge's dramatic works, for it contains characters, situations, and attitudes that we find in his other plays: the contrasting temperaments of the sedentary person and the wanderer; the tramp as emblem of the independent, a-social existence; the loneliness one feels when his life does not 'center' on anything; the power of language to colour, perhaps to remake, reality. But the more general purpose we are exploring, even if separable from the particular content of the plays, is nevertheless important, and we shall see some form of it in each of the plays.

I spoke earlier of Synge's reading of Darwin as a crisis of perspective and stressed that a drastic change of perspective can require the re-evaluation of a whole range of experience – a difficult, potentially traumatic, undertaking. I also suggested that Synge's Aran Islands experience involved a similar contrast of perspectives, in this case rehabilitative and clarifying rather than traumatic and that out of this Synge came to realize the large, if implicit, role played by our received assumptions. Here in *The Shadow of the Glen* we see the first dramatic fruits of that realization – a dramatic device and a theme traceable to that experience. A part of Synge's aim in this play is to make his audience go through on a small scale the kind of experience he had gone through on the islands. He does this by leading the viewer into the situation through a received, even stereotyped perspective, and then permitting the true lineaments of the situation to emerge. The dramatist's proximate goal is to elicit expectations and then confuse them, to throw us into perceptual – specifically, aesthetic – shock; the further goal is to make us consider how firm the hold, how subtle the forms, of our assumptions and stereotypes.

iii

In contrast to *The Shadow of the Glen,* which aroused the critics' denunciation, *Riders to the Sea* has always been one of Synge's most highly acclaimed plays. It and the *Playboy* have usually vied for first place in the critics' regard, and in the early years, when appreciation of the *Playboy* was clouded by controversy, *Riders to the Sea* frequently came out on top. It has, however, had its detractors. The most frequent, almost the sole, basis of criticism of the play is that it is not successful as tragedy. Conversely, however, others have praised it for being the essence of tragedy. But to a striking degree, the play's value has been judged in terms of how well it fulfills the requirements of this genre.

This issue of generic classification or generic integrity has played a remarkably large part in Synge's criticism. Sometimes it appears in terms of what 'school' Synge himself belongs to, whether realist, naturalist, or symbolist; more frequently it appears as a question about what type or genre the individual plays embody. We have already noted Daniel Corkery's charge that Synge could not decide whether *Shadow of the Glen* was to be comedy or tragedy. The same question appears perennially in discussions of *Playboy. The Well of the Saints* has been objected to because its blatant supernaturalism is incongruous with the realism that Synge had supposedly espoused in his earlier plays. Also, critics of *Deirdre of the Sorrows* have concerned themselves with whether it qualifies as a tragedy. And as we shall see, the problem of genre has arisen even about *The Aran Islands.* But nowhere has the generic issue been so dominating as in discussion of *Riders to the Sea.* Beneath almost every discussion of the play, pro and con, is the assumption that Synge intended the play as a tragedy, and that it must be judged as such. The persistence of this question in Synge criticism is not accidental. It reflects a recurrent quality in Synge's works and in his mind, a scepticism about received categories and received ways of seeing that can be related to his Aran Islands experience.

While Synge was probably aware that the play would be approached in these terms, I suggest that he set out not to write a tragedy, but to do something simpler and more difficult: to write a drama without regard to generic categories or philosophical ideologies. His aim was a veridical depiction of a typical episode in the lives of the Aran people, one involving not merely objects and events, but attitudes and responses, and the very quality of their life. He wished to do justice to the strangeness of the archaic milieu he had found on the islands, and to give his audience the opportunity or challenge to empathize into a world view they had never personally known.

That critics have so persistently approached the play as tragedy testifies both to the inescapability of our treating whatever we meet through familiar categories and to the subtlety of the challenge that the play affords. If genre criticism is to be more than procrustean classification, we must be flexible in applying the traditional types to any new work. But as Hugh Fausset says in an essay entitled 'Synge and Tragedy', 'There is a natural tendency among men who are more interested in speculation than in practice to impose standard theory upon art, instead of continually abstracting theory anew from the actual matter before them.'[19] This imposition of theory, of generic type, upon art describes what has happened in most criticism of *Riders to the Sea*.

What Synge attempted in *Riders to the Sea* may be clarified by some perceptive comments that Donna Gerstenberger has made, not about the play, but about the book it is so closely akin to, *The Aran Islands*. Gerstenberger's comments show, first of all, that the problem of generic classification has perturbed critics not only about Synge's plays, but about this work as well, for she says, 'Much of the confusion expressed by critics attempting to deal with the accomplishment of *The Aran Islands* rises out of a failure to understand the *kind* of book it is. The book has been variously described as a book of essays, a travel book, or as notebooks; and, in the case of more discreet but perhaps equally uncomfortable critics, the question of *kind* has been sidestepped altogether.' She goes on, 'Actually, *The Aran Islands* may best be viewed as a work analogous to the documentary, a term which has been given its meaning by the motion picture (a medium not known to Synge during his lifetime), including one made about the Aran Islands by Robert Flaherty, who said that Synge taught him what to see. Synge himself does not attempt to define a genre for his book; his concern is with reality and the service of truth, a concern endorsed by the form he has chosen for his work.' (*John Millington Synge*, p. 22). While we may not agree that 'documentary' best describes *The Aran Islands*, we shall see the appropriateness of Gerstenberger's points, even the analogy between Synge and Flaherty, to *Riders to the Sea*.

In writing *Riders to the Sea,* Synge, to borrow Gerstenberger's phrase, did not attempt to define a genre for the play, since his concern was with reality and the service of truth. He wished to set aside questions of substantiating or refuting any philosophical position or any generic norm in favor of simply being faithful to the quality of life on the islands. In its action and setting this play reflects the Aran Islands more fully than does any of Synge's others. Its plot derives from various accounts that Synge heard there (see *Collected Works,* III, 249-50), and it is his only play set upon the islands.[20] That Synge wished to present his audience with an accurate picture of island life is further shown by the pains that were taken to get authentic props for the staging of the play.[21] But the 'realism' Synge aimed at was to go beyond accuracy of costuming. In this play he hoped to evoke the *Weltanschauung* of the islands by depicting how the people respond to one of the recurrent crises of their lives, and to represent in the directness of the stage presentation, the directness of experience he felt among the people.

But for many critics this directness of experience has been clouded by the intellectual and aesthetic categories through which they see the play. The ubiquity of the generic question in criticism of *Riders to the Sea* provides an analogue to the situation we found with *The Shadow of the Glen.* There we saw the importance of the presumed aesthetic stereotype in determining the audience's response and in furthering Synge's dramatic purpose. Here something similar is happening, for lurking in the background, determining and qualifying the audience's response, we have, not a traditional situation such as the lover's triangle, but the generic pattern of tragedy. Both of these are preexistent aesthetic patterns and both embody in their different ways implicit assumptions about reality and human behaviour. Tragedy is one of the most persistent, clearly defined, and highly regarded of Western literary genres. As such, it expresses assumptions about reality that have long been operative in Western culture. Not that every 'tragedy' has precisely the same metaphysics as every other, but there are familial, generic similarities among them, and Aristotle did to an impressive degree describe these in the *Poetics.* This mode, and its complementary mode, comedy, have been so long-lived and persistent because they embody received Western assumptions about reality. When we begin thinking about the large questions of man's relationship to nature and to fate, our perceptions inevitably drift toward these genres as natural perspectives. Among the ideas involved in Aristotelian tragedy are some degree of order in the world about us (even if we are not wise enough to see it), and some degree of self-determination, of attitude, if not of action. As Aristotle tells us, it would be decidedly un-tragic to see a bad man prosper, or to see a truly good man suffer, because such situations would be repugnant to the view of reality that tragedy involves.[22]

The world-view behind Synge's play is not Aristotelian, but it was not meant to be. It is pagan and archaic, pre-Western and pre-tragic. The view of nature in the play involves not the sense of order behind it, or the possibility of a benign God controlling it, but its power, its inscrutability, its apparent indifference to human concerns. This is not what the Western mind is accustomed to seeing. Greek tragedy, Christian theology, scientific empiricism, however different in other respects, all present nature as ordered, with patterns at least partly discernible by man and conformable to him.[23] We do not find that in *Riders to the Sea*.

Before discussing the world-view of the play, let us sample some responses to it, to see how persistent has been the assumption that it must be judged as tragedy, and some of the results. The response of one of Synge's most astute contemporaries, James Joyce, offers an early and a clear example of this attitude. Synge and Joyce met only a few times; their most important meeting – and the only one documented to any degree – was in Paris in March 1903. At this time Synge did have some semblance of success, or at least of recognition and encouragement from Yeats and Lady Gregory, whereas Joyce had none. Joyce was jealous of any potential rival for the literary messiahship he aspired to, and Richard Ellmann is doubtless right when he says of Joyce's response to *Riders to the Sea*, 'No manuscript was ever read with less sympathy.'[24] Joyce wrote to his brother Stanislaus that 'ever since I read it, I have been riddling it mentally till it has [not] a sound spot'. (Ellmann, *James Joyce*, p. 129). But our interest is in the form Joyce's criticism took: he castigated the play because it failed to measure up to Aristotle's criteria for tragedy. Joyce objected to the catastrophe because it was brought about by a horse rather than by the sea, he objected to the play's brevity, and he said that it was a tragic poem, not a drama. His conclusion to Stanislaus was 'thanks be to God, Synge isn't an Aristotelian'. (Ellmann, *James Joyce*, p. 129).

Joyce's blatant demand that the play conform to Aristotle or be judged a failure prompts the natural rejoinder – Why must we presume that the play is intended to be Aristotelian? Why cannot it stand or fall on its own terms? These are appropriate questions, but critics of the play rarely pause to consider them; for the same assumptions we see so clearly in Joyce underlie, if less obviously, almost all criticism of the play. Interestingly, Synge did not answer Joyce's charges by arguing for any Aristotelian, or even any tragic, qualities in the play; his reply was simply, '"It's a good play, as good as any one-act play can be".' (Ellmann, *James Joyce,* p. 129). But Joyce's concern with seeing the play in Aristotelian terms blinded him to whatever good qualities it had in its own right.[25]

Many other critics have followed Joyce's procrustean lead, presuming the play to attempt tragedy and castigating it for failing. For example, Hugh Fausset terms the play 'the most relentlessly melancholy and yet the least tragic of his plays', and says that 'Such a one-sided conflict is pitiful beyond words, but humanity is too dwarfed a participator in the contest, the ideal is too slenderly opposed to the natural for tragedy of a high significance.' (Fausset, 'Synge and Tragedy', pp. 268-69). Fausset is not saying that such things as the drowning of the sons do not happen, or that a person such as Maurya might not make the response Maurya makes; he is rather presuming that the play intends to dramatize certain Western ideas, that it aims to be 'tragedy of a high significance', and misses. Similarly, Raymond Williams says 'In *Riders to the Sea* the people are simply victims; the acceptance is not whole, but rather a weary resignation. . . . The tragedy is natural, in the most common sense of that term; it is, further, *simply an issue of observation and record. . . .* the emotion of the work is pathetic rather than tragic.'[26] The phrase I have italicized supports my contention that the primary aim of this play is depiction, and that Williams himself saw this, but rejected it as an adequate dramatic aim. Interestingly, this paragraph is considerably revised and the criticism of the play ameliorated in the 1968 revision of Williams' book.

Denis Donoghue explicitly focuses this problem when he says, 'The "plot" of *Riders to the Sea* and the fact that it is capable of being described by no convenient alternative word to "tragedy" makes it necessary to clarify our conception of the tragic experience.' Donoghue, however, himself fails to put the experience of the play first and generic considerations second, for he concludes that '"Riders to the Sea" is not a tragedy: to see the play is to feel a pathetic rather than a tragic experience', and he questionably invokes another Western stereotype when he describes Maurya's state at the end of the play as 'Christian Acceptance'.[27]

Other critics have accepted the basic premise that the play

must be approached as tragedy, but have found justification, sometimes tenuous, for defending it. Thomas F. Van Laan proclaims 'But the play is tragic', though he must find the resolution of the tragedy not in the characters, but in the author: 'Synge has achieved perception, and in the fullness of that perception, no matter how frightening the prospect discovered, lies the resolution of tragedy.'[28] David R. Clark shows a similar concern to vindicate the genre when he asks, 'Is the play too passive in suffering?' and when he concludes that it does qualify as tragedy: 'But if we judge by effect alone, I think we still have to call this little play one of the great modern tragedies because it has that effect of tragic catharsis which Aristotle described as the specific effect of tragedy.'[29]

Another interesting response is that of Una Ellis-Fermor, who notes 'a curious absence of metaphysical or religious implication in the tragedies' *Riders to the Sea* and *Deirdre*, and says that this

> gives to Synge's two tragedies something hard, abrupt, pagan. He shapes a fragment of life, man's and nature's intermingled, a fragment charged with passions that beat against fate, and, giving it clear form, leaves it isolated. . . . This puts his two tragedies in a peculiar position, for though their potency is unquestionable they have not, what great tragedy almost invariably carries with it, the implication of resolution. They are splendid, isolated fragments of human experience, but the human spirit in them, though itself of a high poetic or imaginative quality, is unrelated to any other spiritual value. . . . It may be that the synthesis of Synge's mind is not so complete as we at first supposed. . . .[30]

But I cannot agree that even so purely 'expository' a play as this one lacks metaphysical or religious implications. The problem, I think, is that its metaphysical implications do not run along received Western lines of thought, so that anyone who comes to the play expecting traditional ideas, as Ellis-Fermor does, will be disappointed or puzzled. Her sense that the play is fragmentary and lacks implication, her use of the term *pagan* – even her suggestion that Synge's mind is incapable of synthesis – reflect not a flaw in the play or in Synge's intellect, but her own difficulty in recognizing Synge's intention to do something different in the play than she, and most Westerners, expects.

In each of these instances, the critic's response is colored or distorted by an assumption he brings to the play. But in contrast to

The Shadow of the Glen, where the clash between expectation and presentation was sharp and produced anger or denunciation, here the result is simply a body of criticism largely inappropriate to the work it discusses.

The question of whether the play is tragedy is intimately related to the world-view it projects. This too has been the object of considerable discussion, and has puzzled and even angered some critics. The source of this reaction is, as with the question of tragedy, a difficulty in fitting the *Weltanschauung* of the play into any of the readily received categories of Western culture. For the world-view of the play is a strange amalgam of Christian and pagan (or, to some, of naturalistic and supernatural) that resists easy compartmentalization.

Many critics have noted the presumed rivalry in the play between two world-views – between the rational and Christian view that nature does involve order and has some regard for human needs, and the 'pagan' view of nature as sheer indifferent power. The former is represented by the younger women's hope and prayer and by the young priest who speaks for the Christian world view. Early in the play Nora quotes the priest as saying: "'I won't stop him [Bartley]," says he, "but let you not be afraid. Herself does be saying prayers half through the night, and the Almighty God won't leave her destitute," says he, "with no son living".'[31] Later, after Bartley has left Maurya and has seen Michael's ghost, Cathleen begins to keen and says, 'It's destroyed we are from this day. It's destroyed, surely,' to which Nora responds, 'Didn't the young priest say the Almighty God won't leave her destitute with no son living?' But Maurya says simply, 'It's little the like of him knows of the sea'. (*Coll. Works,* III, 19, 21).

In this foiling of the priest against the sea, we have a foiling of world views, the first representing a reasonable benevolent God, the second representing a sheer power that is man's source, sustainer, and destroyer, and that must be accepted, not understood. In this context, Bartley's drowning virtually undercuts the world view expressed by the priest. The relative position accorded these two views is suggested when Maurya ministers to Bartley's corpse:

Give me the Holy Water, Nora, there's a small sup still on the dresser. [NORA *gives it to her.* MAURYA *drops Michael's clothes across* BARTLEY'S *feet, and sprinkles the Holy Water over him.*] . . . It isn't that I haven't prayed for you, Bartley, to the Almighty God. It isn't that I haven't said prayers in the dark night till you wouldn't know what I'd be saying; but it's a great rest I'll have now, and it's time surely. It's a great rest I'll have now, and great sleeping in the long nights after Samhain, if it's only a bit of wet flour we do have to eat, and maybe a fish that would be stinking. [*She kneels down again, crossing herself, and saying prayers under her breath.*] (*Coll. Works*, III, 25; italics, brackets, ellipses, are in the *Coll. Works* text).

The sprinkling of holy water over the sea-drenched corpse suggests the meagre power of Christianity to assuage the stark reality these people know, and the metaphysical question focused by the priest's claims seems settled in favor of a darker, non-rational view.

But in spite of the almost inescapable inclination to see the Christianity-paganism issue in either-or terms, the play does not present it so simply. It suggests that the Christian view is not so much rejected as subsumed into something larger. This appears most clearly through the actions and attitudes of Maurya. She knows the inexorable, inexplicable power of the sea, and her tranquility at the play's end stems more from exhaustion and resignation than from either Christian Acceptance or tragic dignity.[32] But Maurya has prayed for him repeatedly, and she does sprinkle Bartley with holy water; she is Christian and doubtless she hopes for the truth of its gospel. However much we may wish to cast her as either pagan or Christian, she feels no such division. She is both, blending attitudes that may to us seem incongrous or illogical, but that she does not in the least sense that way. She says that the priest knows little of the sea, not in refutation of the religion he represents, but simply because her experience tells her that the sea is capable of great indifference or cruelty.[33]

Just as Synge did not set out to write an orthodox tragedy, neither did he intend to vindicate or to undercut either a Christian or a pagan view of reality, or even to show the necessary opposition of the two. His purpose was rather to present as faithfully as he could the world-view he found on the islands, and to challenge us to empathize with a perspective that eludes our ordinary categorizations.

But if the play does not conform to Christianity or to the tragic view or even to the rationalist's belief in implicit order, if it depicts instead the sheer, inhuman powers of nature, might it not be an example of a common contemporary genre, naturalism? In its dwelling on realistic detail, on concrete setting, on powers indifferent to man, does not this play have much in common with the works of Crane or Dreiser? The fact is, of course, that it does not, though here too some critics have attempted to force the play into this category or have faulted it for its failure to meet these criteria. That the play does elude naturalism is largely a tribute to Synge's ability to achieve a realism of spiritual milieu as well as of physical detail. This supra-naturalistic verisimilitude also rebuts the charges that Synge was indifferent or insensitive to religious feelings. Many another writer of Synge's day, given the physical severity of the islands' life and the elusiveness and complexity of the people's religious attitude, would doubtless have fallen back on something like naturalism to depict 'how things were'.

Synge, however, was capable of a more radical empiricism. The play contains elements that are supernatural, but that are not Christian: elements that do not conform to any orthodox religious belief, nor to any rationalism, nor certainly to naturalism. Maurya makes passing reference to 'the day Bride Dara seen the dead man with the child in his arms' (*Coll. Works,* III, 19) as if it were commonly accepted knowledge. More important, before she knows of Michael's death, she sees him riding on the pony behind Bartley, in new clothes that suggest that he has already been to a new world and has come back to claim his brother. In such a context, what are we to make of Bartley's death? We can perhaps consider Maurya's vision a fantasy and call Bartley's death a coincidence and an accident. That would satisfy our rationalism or naturalism, but would blandly ignore an essential dimension of the play. And if we accept Michael's ghost and believe that it claimed Bartley, we are transported into a mode of the supernatural that is uncomfortably foreign to Christian orthodoxy. What then are we to make of these aspects of the play? Did Synge himself believe that such things could happen? What genre or literary mode do they throw us into? What we are to make of them is a faithful picture of how things were on the Aran Islands. They are there in the play because they were there in the experience of the islanders. What genre or world view they illustrate, whether tragedy or naturalism or fantasy, paganism or Christianity, is not Synge's concern. If he wishes to evoke such questions at all, it is not because there is a ready answer, but because of what we will learn by wrestling with the questions.

In this context, Malcolm Pittock's is one of the most interesting responses to the play. He acknowledges that many critics feel an unsatisfactoriness in the play that is usually ascribed to an absence of tragic conflict, but suggests that the trouble lies elsewhere, namely in Synge's presentation of the beliefs of the community. Synge's fault, according to Pittock, is that he 'cheats us, for the sake of effect, into actively assenting to some of [the] least acceptable elements' of the islanders' pattern of belief. Pittock goes on,

> Perhaps the most significant falsity in the play is Maurya's vision. Here Synge does not allow us to question the validity of her or her family's belief in its prophetic nature or its relationship to Bartley's death: indeed much of the effect of the play depends on our sharing the islanders' convictions in the matter. It is however, one thing for Maurya to see a vision and to believe that vision fulfilled, but quite another for a modern audience, formed in a different cultural pattern, to believe in such superstition with any real seriousness. But, of course, Synge is building on one of our emotional habits: that we are prepared in return for sensational excitement to pretend to believe in the truth of omens and visions particularly as there is a primitive part of us which can never quite shake such a belief off. Many thrillers involve this kind of bargain with the reader. It is on this level, for in our culture there can be no other, that the audience responds to Maurya's vision of Bartley's death.[34]

This is indeed a strange criticism of Synge, for while others have censured him for indifference or insensitivity to religious attitudes, Pittock faults him for presenting the religious milieu of these people so persuasively that even a 'modern' observer cannot escape it. But surely we should regard Synge's refusal to betray or simplify Maurya's vision and the milieu of belief that underlies it as achievement rather than fault – as an opportunity to, however briefly, see the world through a qualitatively different perspective than the one our modern culture enforces. Pittock's criticism shows clearly that Synge has indeed presented for us a milieu challengingly different from our own.

When Synge went to the Aran Islands, he found a world that was, in terms of his earlier modes of thought, unique and unaccountable. Part of his response to that world was to try to represent it dramatically. Whether this involved his saying to himself, 'Tragedy will not do here, nor will Christian orthodoxy, nor pagan acceptance – I must elude them all,' is doubtful. But he must have known implicitly that no set of categories available to himself or his audience would suffice to exhaust, or even to describe, what he had seen. He owed it to that milieu, to himself, even to his audiences, to provide the opportunity for others to experience, if only by aesthetic reflection, what he had experienced.

In *Riders to the Sea,* Synge has raised questions about the relationship between our abstractions and reality. Here, instead of evoking and frustrating a stereotype as in *The Shadow of the Glen,* he simply depicts, as truly and without predilection as possible, a situation inherently strange to a modern Westerner, and he allows us to make of it what we will. Almost inevitably, we respond to what he has presented in received, traditional terms, in terms of tragedy or Christianity or naturalism, often not only presuming these abstractions to be appropriate to the play, but condemning it if it fails to illustrate them. Apparently, modifying our frames of reference to fit a new experience is as hard as readjusting a shattered stereotype.[35]

iv

In Synge's first two plays, we have seen him presenting his audiences with challenges to the received or stereotyped ways that their 'aesthetic set' predisposed them toward the works. In *The Shadow of the Glen* he did this by evoking a familiar plot-character stereotype and then allowing the true lineaments of the situation to emerge. In *Riders to the Sea* he did it by presenting faithfully a milieu that does not conform to our Western conceptualizations. While it is true that *The Tinker's Wedding* was thought to be potentially offensive to Irish audiences and it was refused production by the Abbey for fear it would provoke trouble, the offending element was hardly so subtle or complex as to deserve description as a challenged aesthetic disposition. The only stereotype Synge might be said to be challenging here is that of the sanctity of the priest. It was feared that the Irish audiences would not tolerate seeing a man of God beaten and sacked by a bunch of tinkers. But if the audience had rioted at the priest's being abused by the tinkers, they would have misdirected their anger. Whatever meaningful challenge the play offers to the priestly image comes not from his being beaten – the poor man cannot be held responsible for that – but from the worldliness he has displayed in his dealings with the tinkers earlier in the play. Our interest in this play lies, however, not in its repetition of a device we have seen in the earlier plays, but in certain situations and themes developed within the play.

If we look within the play we find the theme of abstraction and reality dramatized in the experience of the young tinker woman, Sarah, who in the course of the play learns a great deal about 'cultural relativism' and the intangibility of ideals. Whether she could articulate what she has learned is not the point – probably she could not – but she has learned the speciousness of mere abstractions and the difficulty of transferring them from one culture to another. For the dramatic and psychological interest of the play grows largely out of the interplay of two cultures poised against one another: that of the itinerant tinkers who seem to have no culture, or who define themselves by contrast with that other, orthodox culture, here represented by the priest. The foiling of these two is set up in the opening scene: '*In the background, on the left, a sort of tent and ragged clothes drying on the hedge. On the right a chapel-gate.*'[36] The implicit contrast pervades the play.

The dramatic situation focuses upon one important contrast between the two cultures   their attitudes toward the institution and ceremonies of marriage. The play is set in motion by Sarah's idea that she wants to do as the ladies do and marry her man, complete with ring (of sorts), priest, and ceremony. The progress of this idea in Sarah's mind is the main basis of the play's psychological interest and thematic continuity. We note that neither of the other tinkers thinks much of Sarah's idea. Michael sees it as trivial and bothersome and goes along with it only to keep peace in the family. Mary, the older woman, grasps more fully what is going on in Sarah's mind, but she too regards it as foolish. Michael sees this new idea of Sarah's as a whim, related to recent changes of the moon, that will as quickly pass away, and Mary suggests the same.[37] There is, however, more to it than that, and perhaps more than Michael is capable of seeing until some life-crisis grips him. For Sarah is in a life-crisis, and her turning to the possibly magical effects of the ceremony of marriage reflects that. This is suggested by several of her statements about what she hopes for from being married, and it comes into the open in the play's thematic climax. Note Sarah's appeal to the priest: 'And what time will you do the thing I'm asking, holy father? for I'm thinking you'll do it surely, and not have me growing into an old, wicked heathen like herself.' (*Coll. Works,* IV, 21). The priest assumes that Sarah's emphasis falls on her hopes that the ceremony will redeem her from being a 'wicked heathen', and he replies, 'I'll marry you for [ten shillings and a can], though it's a pitiful small sum; for I wouldn't be easy in my soul if I left you growing into an old wicked heathen the like of her.' (*Coll. Works,* IV, 23). But it is not heathendom Sarah is concerned to escape, and the adjective *old* is more than simply an intensive. Sarah admits that 'spring-time is a queer time, and it's queer thoughts maybe I do think at whiles' (*Coll. Works,* IV, 7), and the queer thoughts going through her head now turn on her own beauty and how quickly she will lose it. In Mary she has constantly before her the image of what she will all too soon become, an old woman wandering on the roads. Her life with Michael and Mary has begun to seem dull and ordinary, and she feels herself moving quickly toward old age. As a result, she turns in her dissatisfaction to that other world the tinkers have always lived beside – the world of ladies, of houses, of stability, of cere-monies – and she endows one of its ceremonies with almost magical powers. She decides that *marriage* will give her life some quality it now lacks.

Whether this is what Sarah really wants is doubtful, for she is a tinker by nature and by choice, and she is probably largely satis-fied with that life. As D. H. Lawrence points out, we are continu-ally subject to both trivial desires and profound desires, and it is not easy, especially in times of crisis, to distinguish them.[38] Sarah looks at Mary and sees her own life rushing toward age and the hardship of a hand-to-mouth existence. We can hardly expect her to see at this time what a strong, even admirable, woman Mary is. For Mary is aware of ageing and hardship, and she has in all likelihood gone through crises of dissatisfaction and fear similar to Sarah's. But Mary has reconciled herself to life as the tinkers know it, and she accepts it fully. She too is curious about the ways of settled society and the orthodox church – she would like to hear a 'real priest saying a prayer' (*Coll. Works,* IV, 21) – but she attributes to the rites of that society none of the special, almost magical quality that Sarah invests them with. She knows that the settled society has its ways and the tinkers have theirs, but that they are worlds apart, and there is little point trying to make the ways of the one fit the other. She knows too that beneath the trappings of the societies, human nature is fairly constant, and the problems people face do not vary nearly so much as the devices they use to palliate them. It is amusing how easily Mary's appeal to the priest to share a drink with her touches the man beneath the cassock and brings out his own complaints about his hard life, what with running back and forth to say Mass and trying to satisfy the bishop. Mary must know, too, that the ceremonies and institutions of society and the church are not magical or absolutely true, but are their own devices for dealing with the perennial problems of temporality and death. The song she sings tells us this:

> And when we asked him what way he'd die,
>   And he hanging unrepented,
> 'Begob,' says Larry, 'that's all in my eye,
>   By the clergy first invented.'
>
> (*Coll. Works,* IV, 17)

Orthodox folk may have the consolations of the church to ease them through old age and death; the tinkers find their own ways of coping with them.

These issues are brought together in the crisis of the play. Michael shows signs of being infected by Sarah's fantasies about society's rituals, expressing fear that she may leave him if he does not marry her, but Mary begins to set both of them straight:

MARY.   And you're thinking it's paying gold to his reverence would make a woman stop when she's a mind to go?

SARAH   [*angrily*]. Let you not be destroying us with your talk when I've as good a right to a decent marriage as any speckled female does be sleeping in the black hovels above, would choke a mule.

MARY.   [*soothingly*]. It's as good a right you have surely, Sarah Casey, but what good will it do? Is it putting that ring on your finger will keep you from getting an aged woman and losing the fine face you have, or be easing your pains, when it's the grand ladies do be married in silk dresses, with rings of gold, that do pass any woman with their share of torment in the hour of birth, and do be paying the doctors in the city of Dublin a great price at that time, the like of what you'd pay for a good ass and a cart? [*She sits down.*]

SARAH   [*puzzled*]. Is that the truth?

(*Coll. Works,* IV, 35, 37)

Sarah is taken aback by Mary's forthright statement, for she had expected something special from her ceremony. Though it takes her some time to accept what Mary has said, the process of her seeing society's rituals for what they are has been set into motion, and it soon works itself out. Sarah tries to maintain her belief in the special efficacy of the priest and the marriage ceremony, but when the father wrongly accuses her of having tried to trick him, all of her misgivings are precipitated. Her attack on him expresses more than anger at being accused of duplicity. It expresses also her disappointment and frustration at her inability to find what she had hoped for in his rituals. She realizes that she is a tinker, and that her only defenses against life are those of the tinkers – a direct and willing acceptance of each day as it comes, in full awareness of its transiency and of the approach of old age and death. She must take Mary as her model, and not a bad one at that. The older woman becomes their spokesman when she says to the sacked priest:

> That's a good boy you are now, your reverence, and let you not be uneasy, for we wouldn't hurt you at all. It's sick and sorry we are to tease you; but what did you want meddling with the like of us, when its a long time we are going our own ways – father and son, and his son after him, or mother and daughter, and her own daughter again – and it's little need we ever had of going up into a church and swearing – I'm told there's swearing with it – a word no man would believe, or with drawing rings on our fingers, would be cutting our skins maybe when we'd be taking the ass from the shafts, and pulling the straps the time they'd be slippy with going around beneath the heavens in rains falling. (*Coll. Works,* IV, 47).

Mary's comment shows that the tinkers do indeed have their own society and their own kinds of tradition.

As the play draws to an end, a clearer-eyed Sarah puts her ring onto the priest's finger and says, 'There's the ring, holy father, to keep you minding of your oath until the end of time; for my heart's scalded with your fooling; and it'll be a long day till I go making talk of marriage or the like of that.' (*Coll. Works,* IV, 49). And Mary again is the one who sets them right about their own mode of life when she says, 'She's vexed now, your reverence; and let you not mind her at all, for she's right surely, and it's little need we ever had of the like of you to get us our bit to eat, and our bit to drink, and our time of love when we were young men and women, and were fine to look at.' (*Coll. Works,* IV, 49).

Along with this rounding out of the psychology and theme we have been tracing, there is an amusing, almost capricious, twist at the play's end. Mary half-seriously suggests, 'Maybe he'd swear a mighty oath he wouldn't harm us, and then we'd safer loose him.' (*Coll. Works,* IV, 47). Though she has earlier expressed curiosity about hearing a real priest say a prayer, she has consistently been sceptical about the priest's modes of power. All along we have seen Sarah as duped by the supposed power of the marriage oath and Mary as shrewdly sceptical of it. Now Mary is the one who suggests that the father vow not to harm them. Does she, then, believe in the priest's vows and in his power to harm them? The play is delightfully subtle and true to life on this count, for it shows that clear-eyed scepticism about the ceremonies and abstractions of another culture is not an either/or matter. Mary can see the foolishness of Sarah's ideas about marriage, but not be at all clear whether her own feelings about the priest's mysterious oaths and curses are foolishness or not. When the tinkers scatter before the priest's Latin malediction, they do so in fear of the possible power of this dark language. It is not exactly that they believe in these powers – certainly they do not in any orthodox sense – but there is some question in their minds, and it is better not to take any chances!

NOTES TO CHAPTER IV

1. Daniel Corkery, *Synge and Anglo-Irish Literature* (Dublin and Cork, 1931); T. R. Henn, ed., *The Plays and Poems of J. M. Synge* (London, 1963), p. 27.
2. 'The Shadow of the Glen and the Widow of Ephesus,' *PMLA*, LXII (March 1947), 234. The play has also been criticized by Frank O'Connor, in Lennox Robinson, ed., *The Irish Theatre* (London, 1939), pp. 41-42; and, more pointedly, by Donna Gerstenberger, *John Millington Synge* (New York, 1964), pp. 33-43. The fullest sympathetic analysis is that of Alan Price, *Synge and Anglo-Irish Drama* (London, 1961), pp. 118-26.
3. In a letter to Fay in April 1904, quoted in *Collected Works,* III (London, 1968), p. xxvii.
4. On the reaction to *The Shadow of the Glen,* see Greene/Stephens, pp. 143-54. Maire Nic Shiubhlaigh briefly describes the actors' walkout in *The Splendid Years* (Dublin, 1955), p. 42. Skelton's comment is in *The Writings of J. M. Synge* (London, 1971), p. 18. Of Synge's draft of the *Play of '98,* Yeats said, 'The play was neither written nor performed, and neither then nor at any later time could I discover whether

Synge understood the shock that he was giving. He certainly did not foresee in any way the trouble that his greatest play brought on us all. (*The Autobiography of William Butler Yeats* [New York, 1965], p. 385). I am sceptical that Synge was unaware of the effects his works would have, especially since audience shock is a recurrent feature of his drama and since we can relate this to Synge's own psychological development. But any aesthetic intention is complex, and the question of how much of Synge's intention was conscious is not of great moment.

5. This touches on complex questions of the relationship among playwright, audience, and subject matter. I do not imply that disinterestedness is the ideal stance of an audience; whether an audience can be dispassionate about a performance is determined by how personally involved they are in the issues being dramatized. Clearly Synge (as most playwrights) wanted an audience that was involved and could be offended. Some extreme developments in film and theatre in recent years have arisen from the writers' attempts to evoke a vital response from audiences so super-sophisticated that they talk only about 'technique' no matter how personal or violent the subject matter.

6. *The Road Round Ireland* (New York, 1926), p. 361.

7. On perceptual set, see Floyd H. Allport, *Theories of Perception and the Concept of Structure* (New York, 1955), especially chapters 9, 10, 11, 15, and 16. For a variety of experiments illustrating set, see the work of A. Ames, Jr. and G. L. Freeman, cited by Allport.

8. The performance was given at the South Atlantic Modern Language Association meeting in Atlanta, Georgia, November 1971.

9. Quoted in Greene/Stephens, pp. 146-47. My italics.

10. The phrase I have italicized is vague, but it must refer to Michael rather than to the tramp. Greene too presumes this, saying 'The reviewer was inaccurate when he described Nora as absconding with her young suitor – she was thrown out by her husband and went off with the tramp after her lover had abandoned her' (Greene/Stephens, p. 147).

11. These comments are quoted or summarized in Greene/Stephens, pp. 147-49.

12. *John Millington Synge* (New York, 1965), p. 13.

13. D. H. Lawrence, 'Art and Morality', in *Phoenix* (London, 1936), pp. 521-26.

14. In *Collected Works*, III, xviii. The phrase I have italicized links this with the theme of perceptual shock pursued in earlier chapters. See pp. 42-43, 44, 76-77.

15. Confirmation of this is provided by the play 'In a Real Wicklow Glen', by 'Conn', which appeared in the *United Irishman*, October 24, 1903, p. 3. The play, representing what Griffith and his followers would have preferred, is ludicrously pious and patriotic – simply an extended stereotype.

16. Quotations are from the text in the *Collected Works*, vol. III (London, 1968), ed. Ann Saddlemyer. This dialogue is on p. 47.

17. For a summary of the discussions of the play's sources, see Adelaide Duncan Estill, *The Sources of Synge* (Philadelphia, 1939), pp. 3-12. Estill concludes, 'Hence my conviction is that all the necessary sources for this play may be found in *The Aran Islands* and *In Wicklow*' (p. 12). Nothing new about the play's sources has emerged since Estill's monograph. For a convenient gathering of the passages in Synge's prose

that form the backdrop for the play, see pp. 258-60 of *Collected Works*, III.

18. Ann Saddlemyer prints the 'original version' of Pat Dirane's story in *Collected Works*, III, 254-55. It does not differ significantly from the one given in *The Aran Islands*.

19. Hugh l'A. Fausset, 'Synge and Tragedy', *Fortnightly Review*, CXV (February 1, 1924), 258.

20. Stage directions describe the setting simply as 'An Island off the West of Ireland', but references to Galway Fair, to Connemara, and to Donegal's being far to the north leave no doubt of the location.

21. For instance, his getting pampooties and native flannel from friends on the islands. (Greene/Stephens, p. 105).

22. See the *Poetics*, section 13.

23. This idea draws upon the similarities Whitehead traces among Greek Fate, medieval theology, and scientific empiricism in the first chapter of *Science and the Modern World* (New York, 1967); see especially pp. 10-13.

24. Richard Ellmann, *James Joyce* (New York, 1959), p. 129.

25. Joyce did, however, come to regard the play more highly and paid it the compliment of translating it into Italian. There have been several critics who first condemned the play for failure as tragedy, but who later came to see it in its own terms and to value it more highly.

26. Raymond Williams, *Drama from Ibsen to Eliot* (London, 1952), p. 160.

27. Denis Donoghue, 'Synge: "Riders to the Sea": A Study', *University Review*, I (Summer 1955), 57, 58.

28. Thomas F. Van Laan, 'Form as Agent in Synge's *Riders to the Sea*', *Drama Survey*, III (Winter 1964), 365.

29. David R. Clark, 'Synge's "Perpetual 'Last Day' "': Remarks on *Riders to the Sea*', in S. B. Bushrui, ed., *Sunshine and the Moon's Delight* (Gerrards Cross and Beirut, 1972), p. 50. Substantially the same essay had appeared as the Introduction to Clark's edition of *Riders to the Sea* (1970).

30. Una Ellis-Fermor, *The Irish Dramatic Movement*, rev. ed. (London: Methuen & Co., 1954), p. 185.

31. Quotations from *Riders to the Sea* are from the *Collected Works*, III (Oxford, 1968). The quoted passage is on p. 5.

32. The first term is used by Denis Donoghue, *op. cit.*, p. 52; the second by William W. Combs in 'J. M. Synge's *Riders to the Sea*: A Reading and Some Generalizations', *Papers of the Michigan Academy of Science, Arts, and Letters*, L, 1965, p. 603.

33. Robin Skelton, under the impetus of the idea that Synge is 'anti-clerical', succumbs to the either/or mentality and attempts to expunge Christianity from the play. He even contends that the Holy Water is pagan, that Maurya collects it only in the nights after Samhain, and says, 'Thus the Holy Water is much more the magical water of pre-Christian belief than the water blessed by the priest. Indeed, the priest is not in it at all'. (*Writings of J. M. Synge*, p. 51).

34. Malcolm Pittock, '*Riders to the Sea*', *English Studies*, XLIX (Oct. 1968), 448-49.

35. There is an interesting analogy between the responses to this play and to Robert Flaherty's film *Man of Aran*. (Donna Gerstenberger has quoted Flaherty's statement that Synge taught him what to see, and

has suggested that Synge's *The Aran Islands* might be approached as a 'documentary'.) Flaherty, like Synge, was fascinated by the uniqueness of the life he found on the islands, and was challenged to convey its quality to his audience without bending his depiction to any contemporary ideology. Yet so difficult did the critics find it to accept such an aim, that Flaherty's film was criticized by the British Board of Film Censors for showing poverty on the screen, at the same time the leftists were attacking the film for its escapism and its failure to depict the class-struggle! (See Arthur Calder-Marshall, *The Innocent Eye: The Life of Robert J. Flaherty* [New York, 1966], pp. 163, 166.)

36. Quotations from *The Tinker's Wedding* are from the *Collected Works,* IV (1968). The passage quoted here is from IV, 7. Subsequent page references are given parenthetically.

37. Robin Skelton takes an opposite approach to this, arguing that the association of Sarah's desire with the changes of the moon suggests that it grows out of deep, pagan sources (*The Writings of J. M. Synge,* pp. 75-76). But the play bears out what Michael implies – that it is a mere whim, as changeable as the moon. Doubtless some of Sarah's feelings spring from deep sources but this desire for orthodox marriage is not one of those. It makes more sense to see this desire as abstract and superficial, an attempt on Sarah's part to adapt to her own situation ideas from another milieu.

38. See 'Apropos of Lady Chatterley's Lover', in *Lady Chatterley's Lover* (London, 1961), esp. pp. 26ff.

V

Dreamer's Vexation or Poet's Balm?: *The Well of the Saints* and *The Playboy of the Western World*

i

As we turn to *The Well of the Saints* and *The Playboy of the Western World*, we move into fuller scale, more philosophical dramatizations of the implications behind what Synge learned from his Aran Island experiences. Several of the devices and situations seen in earlier plays naturally reoccur, especially in *Playboy*, but our interest will turn more sharply on how these two plays express a new phase of Synge's development and on their complementary explorations of their theme. Both plays dramatize the relationship between reality and abstractions, with particular emphasis upon why some abstractions have the power to modify reality, while others offer at best a deceitful and dangerous delusion. Their presentation of these issues is not simply sociological or psychological, but metaphysical, and the plays propose philosophically complementary treatment of their theme, the first dark and nihilistic, the second more subtle and affirmative. In *The Well of the Saints,* the Douls are shown to be building their lives upon a lie that has no power to modify the reality they cannot accept, a lie that can only delude them. The confrontation between reality and dream is static and futile. In *The Playboy of the Western World,* Christy truly is remade by 'the power of a lie', and we find Synge presenting a more dynamic and satisfying relation between idea and reality. The prime agency by which idea and reality interrelate is language, which assumes in *Playboy* a thematic significance only adumbrated in earlier plays. And in addition to presenting a satisfying expression of this underlying theme, *Playboy* seems in other ways the culmination for Synge of

127

the complex of ideas we have been tracing. Here various themes and devices come together in a way that seems to have been fully satisfying for Synge and to have enabled him to move on to new dramatic terrain. How this is true we shall see in *Deirdre of the Sorrows.*

The critical attention that *The Well of the Saints* has received, though small, shows that the play not only puzzled and offended several early critics, but that it continues to prompt more basic divergence of opinion than any other of Synge's plays. Some critics regard it as darkly pessimistic, or as inconsistent with Synge's own world view; others see it as dramatizing Synge's own nihilism; still others as championing existential freedom. This difference of opinion is of particular interest to us because it grows out of what the play seems to be saying about the relationship between abstractions and reality.

First a look at two early responses. Joseph Holloway's reaction was typical of the feeling the play inspired in Dublin when it was first performed in February 1905. Holloway found the play irreverent and coarse, almost blasphemous, and said,

> Making a jeer at religion and a mock at chastity may be good fun, but it won't do for Irish drama. If there are two things ingrained in the Irish character above all else, they are their respect for all pertaining to their religious belief and their love of chastity, and these are the very subjects Mr Synge has chosen to exercise his wit upon.[1]

In language echoing Griffith's strictures against *The Shadow of the Glen,* Holloway added, 'To call it Irish is distinctly a libel on our race and country' (p. 41). Holloway's denunciation, though, may have been prompted not by the play's lewdness or blasphemy, but by the troubling metaphysical implications he felt within it – implications more clearly sensed and objected to by later critics.

In addition to being faulted for failing to do justice to the piety of the Irish, Synge's play was also criticized for the opposite failing. In a review in *Dana* for March 1905, presumably written by Thomas Keohler, the play was criticized for being based upon a supernatural event, for, Keohler says, 'the very fact of a play being based on an incident of this nature precludes it in a measure from any vital connection with the tendencies and developments of modern life and thought.'[2] He calls this an 'incongruity' on the part of a dramatist who had up until now been realistic, and deplores the effect the play might have if produced before a gullible audience:

> As we all know, there are thousands of people in this country who believe implicitly in the possibility of such a miracle taking place in this particular manner, and if the play should ever happen to be produced in rural districts, it would most likely tend to strengthen this belief, and in so far as it did so, would be allying itself to the already too numerous forces in the land opposed to intellectual progression. (*Dana,* #11, p. 351).

Though Keohler's criticism at first seems quite different from Holloway's – Synge is being criticized for jeering at religion on the one hand and for supernaturalism on the other – the two have much in common. Synge has disappointed both critics by failing to provide something consistent with what they think he should be doing. Holloway is miffed because Synge's play does not illustrate Irish piety and patriotism; Keohler is upset because it does not further intellectual progressivism. Both reactions, then, exemplify the response to Synge's plays that we have seen repeatedly – inability to view the plays apart from some ideology or stereotype they are supposed to support, and frustration because they fail to do so. Holloway's type of criticism – of Synge's religious or political perfidy – was common, and we have already explored its bases. Keohler's seems different but arises from analogous sources. He contends that Synge has always been realistic, and that he now incongruously presents us with a play that cannot be put into that category. But the defection Keohler detects is in his own eye, for Synge never devoted himself to any particular mode, and 'realistic' is, as we have seen, hardly an adequate term for *Riders to the Sea,* where there are references to visions of dead men, and a strange concatenation of events leading to Bartley's death. Keohler's criticism expresses a more basic frustration, for he is a rationalist, a believer in 'intellectual progression', and is disturbed that the play should sanction another world-view. In this respect it is analogous to Malcolm Pittock's criticism of *Riders to the Sea* for asking a modern, rationalistic audience to accept the supernaturalism of the islanders (see above p. 117). We have long known that Synge's dramas did not satisfy contemporary Irish patriots and religionists; now we see that they were also unacceptable to a very different camp – the rationalists.

The striking variety of response among recent critics even more obviously reflects metaphysical differences among them. Consider, for example, the responses of three intelligent critics of Synge – Alan Price, Donna Gerstenberger, and Robin Skelton. Though they approach them in different terms, these critics do agree about the play's themes. For all three, the issue is the relationship between the Douls' dream or belief, and their experience, between imagination and reality – in our terms, between some idea or abstraction they are trying to vindicate, and the reality they are faced with. But the critics' judgements on these themes are quite different. Alan Price, in the fullest discussion of the play, sees it as Synge's most profound work and consistently praises it.[3] Donna Gerstenberger on the other hand criticizes almost every facet of the play and concludes that its ending is untrue to what Synge himself thought about reality.[4] Robin Skelton stresses the Douls' 'inalienable right' to their dream and praises them for creating it.[5]

These critics disagree about the play primarily because they react differently to the implicit metaphysic they find in it, either about the truth of that metaphysic, or about how well it expresses Synge's own beliefs. Price sees nihilism in the play, but can praise it because he believes Synge to have been a nihilist:

> Synge's own view of human life appears to have been a melancholy one. He felt that although everyday existence might be, for most people, tolerable, and even happy at times, life in this universe, stripped of all its comforting camouflage, was in essence meaningless: Man's aspirations, his ideas of love, goodness, beauty, vital though they may be for a few years, all alike find the inevitable end; and beyond the grave there is nothing. Consequently, the few people that see life clearly and see it whole are faced with a ghastly spectacle; one which is spared to the vast majority, who, lacking this insight, are accordingly more or less content and find life well worth living. (Price, p. 138).

For Gerstenberger, however, who sees reality and Synge's view of it differently, the play is unsatisfactory: the Douls' choice 'is one that denies the wholeness of the world, the totality of experience; it also denies what Synge himself had learned about reality'. (Gerstenberger, p. 61). And Skelton praises the creative self-assertion he finds in the drama, saying of Synge's, 'he took what we would now label an existentialist view'. (Skelton, p. 101).

Gerstenberger's analysis is worth scrutiny because she so sharply focuses the thematic issues in the play. It deals, she says, with 'the power of the imagination to create and to destroy, and the compromises men make with reality' (p. 55). But Gersten-berger is disturbed by Synge's development of this theme because 'in this play Synge makes one of the few partial compromises to be found anywhere in his work, for the play ends with a preference for the lie, an insistence upon illusion in place of reality' (p. 55). In the Douls' knowing, intentional choice of blindness over sight, 'They have entered a self-inflicted exile, but it is an exile made with a full awareness of the alternative' (p. 59). Pursuing this, she says, 'The only way to escape the implications of Synge's con-clusion to *The Well of the Saints* is to read the conclusion as an ironic statement that, considering the alternatives, it is a matter of choosing between two lies – the illusion about reality which blindness affords and the figurative blindness of the sighted world in the face of reality' (pp. 55-56). And this she cannot accept, for as we have seen, she sees in the play philosophical implications inconsistent with the truth about reality and with Synge's own presumed world view. From this basic inconsistency, from what she calls the 'lack of real commitment to all the implications of his play' (p. 56), Gerstenberger traces other weaknesses in language and structure.

Gerstenberger's argument presumes the metaphysical nature of the problems the play dramatizes, for she focuses not on an internal inconsistency, but on an inconsistency with what is true, and with what Synge presumably believed. The play shows that the Douls prefer their blindness to sight, even though they know that their dreams of beautiful hair and beard are elaborations on reality so exaggerated as to be lies. But because we sense that the Douls are presented by Synge more sympathetically than the villagers, we seem driven to conclude that Synge stands behind their choice, and that the lie they accept is preferable to the reality of the villagers. But what bothers us about this is that they so obviously know their newly elaborated dream is a lie and an escape. Synge develops the theme so pointedly that we cannot fail to see how great a retreat from reality the Douls' preference for blindness is. We may sympathize when Martin says 'The devil mend Mary Doul for putting lies on me, and letting on she was grand,' which is understandable, but how are we to respond when he immediately adds 'The devil mend the old Saint for letting me see it was lies'?[6] This too is quite human, but we can hardly admire it or take it as a pattern to live by. Their subsequent con-versation is a strange mixture of elaboration of new fantasies, mixed with explicit discussion of and resentment about lies they were earlier subjected to. And after they have begun to bask in the warmth of their new dreams, Mary shows how clearly they see their own lies and their need for blindness by saying 'and what good'll our grey hairs be itself, if we have our sight, the way we'll see them falling each day, and turning dirty in the rain?'. (*Coll. Works,* III, 135). The escapism of their blindness is evident when Martin ironically says to the Saint, 'That's great sights, holy father. . . . What was it I seen my first day, but your own bleeding feet and they cut with the stones, and my last day, but the villainy of herself that you're wedding, God forgive you, with Timmy the smith. That was great sights maybe. . . . And wasn't it great sights seeing the roads when north winds would be driving and the skies would be harsh, and you'd see the horses and the asses and the dogs itself maybe with their heads hanging and they closing their eyes – '. (*Coll. Works,* III, 141; ellipses are in the text).

The implication is clear that Martin prefers not to see these things: he knows them to be true, but if permitted his blindness, he can put them out of his mind. His understanding is also evident in Martin's departing speech, where he says, 'we're going on the two of us to the towns of the south, where the people will have kind voices maybe, and we won't know their bad looks or their villainy at all'. (*Coll. Works,* III, 149). He does not say that the people in the other towns will not *be* bad looking or villainous, but simply that, being blind, the Douls won't *know* their bad looks or villainy. Such a bald admission of the wish to retreat from realities into fantasies should take us aback and make us uneasy about the play's implications.

Here the very different evaluations of Price and Gerstenberger come into play. Price recognizes the escapist, even nihilist, implications, but he concludes that this shows the meaninglessness of life for both the Douls and for Synge, and praises the play as an effective if negative presentation. Gerstenberger, presuming from her knowledge of Synge's other works and statements that he cannot agree with the play's implications, declares it inconsistent with Synge's world view and untrue to reality.

Two points about this critical disagreement deserve notice. First, the issue here truly is metaphysical; it involves the relationship between abstractions or ideals, and reality – the question of how the Douls can continue to view reality through beliefs that they know to be false. Second, those who agree with Gerstenberger that the play is untrue to Synge's own beliefs as inferred from a broader context should consider carefully what they are objecting to, lest they condemn the play for a stance it does not take. For all that Synge shows us in this play is that the Douls are capable of building their lives on a foundation of illusion and untruth. We may, mainly because he presents them sympathetic-ally, infer that he sanctions their actions and is thus untrue to his larger beliefs, but that is an inference on our part. We should ask a question analogous to one we asked about Maurya in *Riders to the Sea:* Are such critics saying that people's lives *never are* built upon illusion and untruth, or that they *should not be?* Any-one who has read much of modern literature, of Conrad, Kafka, or Beckett, knows that no one's life is founded upon stark reality and that we all rely upon a great deal that will not bear scrutiny.

I agree then with Gerstenberger that the Douls build upon an illusion so specious and so blatant that it amounts to a lie, and that this was not Synge's way of looking at things. For these reasons I disagree with Alan Price's contention that the play expresses Synge's nihilism. I disagree even more with Robin Skelton's view of the play, for he clouds the very metaphysical problems Synge wished to explore, by contending that the Douls had every right to their dreams and by regarding their departure as a triumph. Surely the collision between dream and reality here is so stark as to make any talk of their 'right' to it irrelevant. But in spite of Synge's mainly sympathetic presentation of the Douls, I disagree with Gerstenberger's inference that the play intends to dramatize Synge's own world view. I suggest that in this play Synge is exploring, not advocating, what he shows us, and that before we can talk about what Synge himself believed, we must consider the complementary and more subtle and satisfactory presentation of these same themes in *The Playboy of the Western World.* In *The Well of the Saints* we find abstraction and reality colliding with a directness few of us can ignore or accept. But we need not – indeed in view of his subsequent handling of this theme we cannot – presume that it presents Synge's conclusions, but rather his ruminations, his explorations, perhaps his fears. In the severe, static, disjunction between idea and reality we see in Martin and Mary Doul, Synge is showing that some persons do have an amazing capacity to ignore the imperative that our ideas and our experiences should be consonant. He is also showing that there are some facets of reality too adamant to be modified by whatever abstractions we attempt to impose on them. He may also be suggesting that we should be wary of casting the first stone at those who harbor 'irrational' world views, for while few of us would admit any kinship with the Douls, most of us would have to agree with Conrad's Winnie Verloc that 'some things will not bear much looking into'. The dark, nihilistic implications of this play are then a necessary part of Synge's full exploration of the theme of ideas and reality, but they are only a part, as we shall see in *The Playboy of the Western World*.

ii

The Playboy of the Western World has come to be Synge's most highly regarded play, and it is probably his most successful. It has not, however, been universally praised; Donna Gerstenberger even claims that of all Synge's plays, it 'has called forth the most persistently uncomfortable reactions from audiences and critics alike, from the date of its first performance in the Abbey Theatre in 1907 to the present time'. (*John Millington Synge*, p. 75). It was the most hostilely received of all Synge's plays, being met with riots at its first performance in Dublin and in the U.S.[7] Although more recent, less emotionally involved, critics have been able to see the play's virtues more clearly, there are still some dissenting opinions about its success. The reasons lie largely in the *Playboy*'s facing its audience with several of the problems or challenges we have seen in earlier plays.

In terms of the themes and devices we are pursuing through Synge's works, the *Playboy* is his most comprehensive, even his culminating expression. Like *The Shadow of the Glen*, *Playboy* baffles our attempts to fit the characters and events into any easily grasped aesthetic pattern; like *Riders to the Sea*, it frustrates our attempts to place it in a generic classification; like *The Tinker's Wedding*, it presents characters whose own perceptions undergo changes amounting to revolution; like *The Well of the Saints*, it specifically explores the relations between abstractions and reality. *Playboy*, then, is comprehensive, but it is also distinctive, for while it blends all these devices and themes, it goes beyond the earlier plays in depth of insight into the problem of how abstractions and reality interrelate.

That *Playboy* offers its audience some kind of challenge, psychological or aesthetic, is clear from the reception it received and from the variety and depth of explanations that have been offered for this reception. The drama was denounced by reviewers for faults ranging from dirty language and libel upon the Irish character, to psychological inconsistency or opacity, and tonal and generic confusion. The putative reasons for the riots were the depiction of the Irish peasants', especially the women's, apparent worship of this father-killer, and Christy's phrase about 'a drift of chosen females, standing in their shifts itself, maybe'. But even in the early reviews, it was apparent that something deeper disturbed the audiences, and more recent critics have brought a species of depth psychology to bear on the problem. For instance, T. R. Henn says, 'It seems to me likely that the offensive word was no more than a catalyst for the general but indeterminate unease caused by a number of other factors in the play; and these factors in this are themselves complicated by Synge's technique of producing, deliberately, an ebb and flow in the audience's response to character and situation.' (*The Plays and Poems of J. M. Synge,* pp. 61-62). Donna Gerstenberger points in the same direction when she says that we are beginning through Freud and Fraser to understand these reactions to the play. (*John Millington Synge,* p. 75).[8] The play is sufficiently complex that there are many reasons for the responses it has received, but these have stemmed in large part from factors of audience psychology we have already seen operating in the earlier plays, such as frustration at being unable to know what attitude to take toward the central character and toward the play itself.

To illustrate how *Playboy* comprehends earlier themes and devices, we should consider some of the critical statements about *Playboy,* especially as they express puzzlement over Christy, and the related question of the genre the play belongs to. The problems frequently revolve around whether Christy is presented as hero or buffoon, and whether his play is comedy, satire, farce, or what. Maurice Bourgeois summarizes early response when he questions whether Synge is not a playboy playwright who 'chooses as his subject the crudest possible paradox, wherewith he, by a sort of perpetual *double entendre,* authorizes contradictory interpretations of his play and, as Christy did the Mayo countryfolk, constantly and consistently mystifies his public, who apparently have not yet been able to decide whether his "comedy" is a work of serious portraiture or of fanciful tomfoolery?' (*John Millington Synge and the Irish Theatre,* p. 207). The audience's consternation is reflected in other diverse comments, from George Birmingham's admission that the play is 'very difficult to understand, as difficult as Ibsen was at first to English audiences', to John Galsworthy's describing it as Synge's masterpiece and saying, 'What is it for mankind at large? An attack on the Irish character! A pretty piece of writing! An amusing farce! Enigmatic cynicism leading nowhere! A puzzling fellow wrote it! Mankind at large has little patience with puzzling fellows.'⁹ Other early comments reflected this same frustration over how the play was to be taken. It was said to be 'incongruously styled a comedy', that the 'whole affair is absolutely incomprehensible', that there is 'nothing to show that this picture is not to be taken seriously', that after this experience, the majority of playgoers 'will be rather strengthened than otherwise in their preference for the conventional form of stage representation', that the *Playboy* 'is described as a comedy, but its "humor" is of such a low and vulgar type as to disgust, not to amuse, any mind of ordinary refinement and good taste'.¹⁰ D. J. O'Donoghue's response so well illustrates the frustration the play inspired that it deserves fuller quotation:

> As presented at first, I regarded it as a seriously meant contribution to the drama. It now appears as an extravaganza, and is played as such. And yet it lacks the essentials of an extravaganza. The continuous ferocity of the language; the consistent shamelessness of all the characters (without exception), and the persistent allusions to sacred things make the play even more inexcusable as an extravaganza than as a serious play. I prefer to regard it in the latter sense, in justice to Mr Synge's undoubted power as a writer. As a serious play it offends many people; as an extravanganza, it is made peculiarly vile by the many serious allusions to things which Catholic and Protestant hold sacred. (Quoted in Kilroy, *The 'Playboy' Riots,* p. 76, from a letter in the *Freeman's Journal* of Monday, February 4, 1907.)

That Synge was aware of the problems he was causing for his audience and to some extent invited them is suggested by his own comments while the play was being pilloried. In a letter to the *Irish Times* on January 31, 1907, Synge said, '"The Playboy of the Western World" is not a play with "a purpose" in the modern sense of the word, but although parts of it are, or are meant to be, extravagant comedy, still a great deal that is in it, and a great deal more that is behind it, is perfectly serious, when looked at in a certain light. That is often the case, I think, with comedy, and no one is quite sure today whether "Shylock" and "Alceste" should be played seriously or not. There are, it may be hinted, several sides to "The Playboy".' (Quoted in Kilroy, *The 'Playboy' Riots,* p. 41.)

He also said, in a letter to M. J. Nolan on February 19, 1907, that 'I wrote the P.B. directly, as a piece of life, without thinking, or caring to think, whether it was a comedy, tragedy, or extravaganza, or whether it would be held to have, or not have, a purpose. . . .'[11] But as Synge's voluminous and detailed note sheets for the play reveal, this is only partly true. Synge's meticulous attention to the moods he was evoking and foiling against one another show that he must have been aware of such questions, and that he deliberately produced a medley of tones that would confute the usual psychological or generic categories.[12] In fact, the play has a greater tonal complexity than any other Synge wrote, and this contributes to the puzzlement the audience feels.

The problem of the play's genre persists for more recent critics. Una Ellis-Fermor calls the play a 'tragi-comedy' (*The Irish Dramatic Movement,* p. 179); T. R. Henn says *'The Playboy* does not lend itself readily to classification', and refers to it variously as sheer extravagant comedy, as Dionysiac comedy, and as satire (*The Plays and Poems of J. M. Synge,* pp. 56-57). Alan Price says, 'Clearly in *The Playboy* we have the unusual phenomenon of a play which obeys the rules of twentieth-century naturalism and yet produces a fulness of effect hitherto obtained only by dramatists working in conventions more suitable for the poetic dramatist.' (*Synge and Anglo-Irish Drama,* p. 179). And Donna Gerstenberger, in an approach to the play that is similar to my own, says that the shock the play gives its audience is intentional, and that a part of the play's purpose is the 'questioning of the assumptions which make the comic mode possible'. (*John Millington Synge,* pp. 91, 87).

Much of the difficulty in categorizing the play arises out of the ambiguity of the central characters and the complexity of their psychology. Is Christy being presented as a typical peasant, or is he a humorous and exaggerated figure? Are we seriously to believe that the women of this community would flock to a parricide? Are these women presented as types of the Irish peasant? Synge himself did not help to resolve this when, in the midst of the flurry, he cited actual case histories of admired criminals (at least concealed criminals) on the one hand, and declared the play an extravaganza on the other.

Because of the complexity of the psychology, Christy seems to vacillate between cowering and bragging, and at the end of the play he seems different than he was at the beginning. Both the vacillation and the change are of course necessary to the central theme of the young man's self-surprising growth under the influence of the people's expectation and admiration. In the early stages of the play he is merely a potential hero (and potential buffoon, coward, etc.), and his attitude does waver between fear and self-assertion. And at the play's end he *is* different than he was at the beginning, for one of the potential selves latent within him has been evoked and realized. Pegeen's psychology is perhaps even more intricate than Christy's. She vacillates continually in such a way that a viewer might be puzzled and conclude that Synge did not know what he was doing. But as Synge pointed out, there are simple characters and subtle characters, and the subtle ones create problems for both audiences and actors. In his letter to M. J. Nolan, he said, 'Remember on the first production of a play the most suttle [sic] characters always tend to come out less strongly than the simple characters, because those who act the suttle parts can do no more than feel their way till they have acted the whole play a number of times.'[13] Given the advantage of seventy years' hindsight and discussion, we can make sense of Pegeen's psychology. The unevenness of her attitude toward Christy – first adulation and then scorn – expresses both her wish to find out how much of a man she is dealing with, and her uncertainty about whether she most deeply wants to rule or be ruled by her man. The severity of her treatment of him at the play's end expresses her deep disappointment when she concludes that he is much less of a man than she had thought, followed by her even deeper chagrin upon finding that he is worth having, but that she has let him escape her. Viewed along these lines, nothing that she does seems psychologically incongruous.

In short, we have in *Playboy* a work whose complexity of theme and psychology and whose tonal ambiguity, when coupled with its racy language and its toying with the touchy subject of the Irish character, were almost certain to produce dramatic, and negative, response from its original audience. We in our leisure and from our distance can view the play more coolly and pronounce it a masterpiece, charting with pleasure its psychological intricacies, and enjoying rather than being disturbed by its generic and tonal ambiguity. But our present understanding does not invalidate the original response by an audience that was deeply involved in the implications of the work and that felt in some indefinable way their measure was being taken and they were being made fun of.

So far we have considered *Playboy* largely from the viewer's perspective, as a challenging and perturbing experience that forcibly involves the audience in issues of aesthetic predisposition. In this we see the play's similarity with Synge's first three plays. We turn now to the basis for comparing the play with *The Well of the Saints* – its exploration of the philosophical issues within the theme of abstraction and reality. When we see the striking similarity of theme and the more subtle and comprehensive handling it receives in *Playboy,* we can no longer identify the world view implicit within the earlier play as Synge's own.

In *The Well of the Saints* we saw in the Douls' decision to preserve their blindness and elaborate their dreams a direct confrontation between dream and reality, leaving no doubt that the Douls are willing to build their lives upon a lie. In *Playboy* we find the same theme approached and developed very differently, for Christy too has a dream. The basic difference is that in the former play, dream and reality are presented as static and dichotomous; the confrontation between the two is so stark that it provides for nothing but static opposition, with nihilistic implications. The dreams of the Douls are so clearly set against reality, or have so little basis in it, that they must be seen as lies, and critics who face this issue conclude either that Synge is a nihilist or that the play is untrue to Synge's larger perspectives (the responses respectively of Alan Price and Donna Gerstenberger). In *Playboy,* however, Christy tells the people that they are 'after making a mighty man of me this day by the power of a lie.' Here, then, the 'lie' Christy is transformed by is something different than the Douls' 'dream', and so by implication is the 'reality' it transforms.[14]

The metamorphosis of Christy from whining boy to self-confident hero is the main basis of the play's development, and the catalyst in the reaction is the image of Christy in the eyes of the townspeople. During the play he becomes in actuality the hero they mistakenly presumed him to be at the outset. Pegeen's image of him (or his own image of her image) is most important, for his growth occurs largely so that he may become worthy of her. As a result of his aspirations, the reality of what Christy is undergoes a transformation because of the dream it is challenged by.

Several critics have called attention to the eloquence of Christy's language and have traced through the play the growing vigor and imagination of Christy's accounts of his battle with his father, pointing out the importance of his successive elaborations of his story of the slaying and of his rhapsodic wooing of Pegeen in his transformation.[15] I agree with these points and shall not reiterate them, nor shall I dwell upon the admitted beauty and poetry of the play's dialogue. But certain thematic implications of these points do deserve special attention, for here in *Playboy,* language takes on an importance that is at best only hinted at in earlier plays. To appreciate this we must distinguish between the skilful *use* of language, which is a feature of all Synge's plays, and the *theme* of language as we see it here. Synge had from his earliest plays used language skilfully; further, he had suggested, through the tramp's description to Nora of the life they would share, or through the priest's curse, or through Martin Doul's appeal to Molly Byrne, that language could heighten or intensify our experience. But none of the previous plays makes the claim for language that *Playboy* does, for none of them provided a context in which the philosophical implications of the power of language came to the surface. Synge had long been aware of the capacity of language to color experience, and he doubtless knew of the even greater power ascribed to it by early Irish poets – the power to restore lost sight or to cause death. In *Playboy,* Synge's rumination on these ideas and his wrestling with the problem of how abstractions and reality relate come together, and the result is a much more subtle and satisfactory perspective on these issues than that lying behind *The Well of the Saints.*

In *Playboy,* language acts as mediator between actuality and potentiality, between reality and abstraction, for it is largely through language – through his successive accounts of the murder and his self-surprising eloquence in wooing Pegeen – that Christy projects and brings into being one of his potential selves that had until now lain dormant.[16] The implications of this for the question we are considering are important indeed, for they suggest a more complex view of reality than *The Well of the Saints* offered. While some facets of reality are doubtless quite obdurate, not all of it is static, objective, fixed. Some aspects of reality – e.g. human personality – are better understood as a congeries of potentialities waiting to be evoked and realized by the imagination, through the medium of language. This is very different from the impression left by *The Well of the Saints,* where reality and dream are presented as dichotomous and opposed, the one static and concrete, the other static and abstract. In *Playboy* we are asked to see reality as involving potentialities, and the dream or abstraction as the agency by which some of these potentialities are led out and given substance. Martin's dream, conceived in escapism and aimed at transforming his and Mary's wrinkles and grey hair, is doomed to failure; Christy's on the other hand, conceived in hope and aimed at transforming his self, succeeds.

The Well of the Saints and *Playboy* then present us with contrasting dramatizations of the same theme. Can we say that one of the two is truer, or closer to Synge's own view? So stated, the question is simplistic and misleading, but it is still worth considering. The stance dramatized within *The Well of the Saints* is true, in that there are abstractions that belie reality and that are incapable of being reified, and there are some facets of reality so adamant as to be unalterable by hopes or dreams. What *Playboy* presents is not a contradictory view, but a complementary and more comprehensive one. Still aware that reality has its obdurate facets, Synge is exploring here some of the less adamant ones, and showing how these may be influenced by ideas and dreams. In this sense the dream of the Douls is shown to be a 'lie', in that it is too alien to potential reality to alter it, and the 'lie' that Christy believes is a viable dream, in that it can and does modify reality. The problem, of course, is that we cannot easily distinguish the malleable facets of reality from the unmalleable, nor can we foresee whether a given hope is, in Keats's terms, vexation or balm.[17] In any event *Playboy* offers a more subtle and in this sense a truer presentation of this theme than does *The Well of the Saints*. Whether Synge at the time he wrote the earlier play 'believed' the view he presented there, I cannot say. I suspect that the negativism there, the static confrontation between reality and idea, represented one possibility that Synge was aware of, perhaps feared, and that he felt compelled to examine. But in *Playboy* he went deeper, showing that while ideas and dreams may not move mountains, they can change persons, and that in itself is mystery and miracle. ⅹTᏒⲓⲩⲙⲣⲏ

Playboy has been seen by many as a turning point in Synge's career (or *Deirdre* as a new departure, amounting to the same thing). Certainly in terms of the themes we have been tracing through his mind and art, this is true, for the play presents the fullest and most comprehensive presentation of those themes. Here they exist both as challenge to the audience and as dramatized subject matter, and the dramatization presents the theme subtly and effectively. And while this play offers full and varied testimony to the power of implicit abstractions, Synge goes beyond that, to the realization that abstractions can, if properly used, be a subtle means of seeing new aspects of reality, even of altering the nature of reality. Having seen this, Synge came to a sufficiently satisfying vantage point on these issues that, in his next play, he went on to 'apply' what he had learned, in order to find his own individual perspective on the material he was dramatizing.

NOTES TO CHAPTER V

1. *Joseph Holloway's Abbey Theatre* (Carbondale, 1967), p. 41.
2. *Dana*, No. 11 (March 1905), p. 351.
3. Alan Price, *Synge and Anglo-Irish Drama* (London, 1961), pp. 138-61.
4. Donna Gerstenberger, *John Millington Synge* (New York, 1964), pp. 55-62.
5. Robin Skelton, *The Writings of J. M. Synge* (Indianapolis, 1971), pp. 91-103. Nicholas Grene, in *Synge: A Critical Study of the Plays* (Totowa, N. J., 1975) recognizes the theme of 'truth and illusion' in the play and compares it with Ibsen's *The Wild Duck*, Gorki's *The Lower Depths*, and O'Neill's *The Iceman Cometh*. He, as Skelton, speaks of Martin's 'right' to his blindness and says that 'Martin's vision is at once delusion, and imaginative truth' (p. 130). This paradox reflects Grene's interesting claim that, while the drama evokes the question of reality and truth, the fullness of the play enables Synge to get beyond 'the ordinary dualism of truth and illusion' (p. 131). But Grene does not explain how the play's 'serio-comic view of the world' can elude or transcend the basic dilemma.
6. *The Well of the Saints, Collected Works*, III, 125. Subsequent references are given parenthetically.
7. On these riots, see chapter XIII of the Greene/Stephens biography, and James Kilroy's *The 'Playboy' Riots* (Dublin, 1971). Kilroy's pamphlet reprints contemporary newspaper response.
8. For other examples of a depth psychology approach, see Irving D. Suss, 'The "Playboy" Riots', *Irish Writing*, No. 18 (March 1952), 39-42; and Patricia Mayer Spacks, 'The Making of the Playboy', *Modern Drama*, IV (December 1961), 314-23.
9. George A. Birmingham, 'The Literary Movement in Ireland', *Fortnightly Review*, LXXXII (December 2, 1907), 955; John Galsworthy, 'Meditation on Finality', in *The Inn of Tranquility: Studies and Essays* (London, 1912), p. 207.
10. These are from various newspapers reactions, quoted in Kilroy, *The 'Play' Riots*, pp. 7, 9, 10, 11, 21.
11. In *John Millington Synge: Some Unpublished Letters and Documents* . . . (Montreal, 1959), pp. 11-12.
12. William Hart discusses Synge's orchestration of moods in the play in 'Synge's Ideas on Life and Art . . .', *Yeats Studies*, No. 2 (1972), 35-51. This is also confirmed by the worksheets for *Playboy*, printed in vol. IV of the Oxford *Collected Works*; see especially pp. 296-97.
13. *John Millington Synge: Some Unpublished Letters and Documents . . .*, pp. 12-13. One reviewer of the 1912 London performance illustrated the difficulties facing the actors, and the effects their choices could have. He criticized Mr O'Donovan's performance as Christy, saying that it 'tended to pitch the whole conception into the element of farce', and that with few exceptions, 'the whole company followed suit and ignored the richer complexities of the play. The audience fell agape into the net, and intensified what is nothing but a falsification of Synge's

original meaning. The poetry was relegated into an interlude, an irrelevance, a byplay; the tragedy was clouded over; the characterization stereotyped and emasculated. Such are the consequences of allowing delicate comedy to masquerade in the guise of farce.' The reviewer's awareness of the source of this problem in the complex nature of the play is shown by an earlier remark: '*The Playboy* is by no means the simple "comedy" that the majority of London critics would have us believe. Its strands are woven of both comedy and tragedy, patterned into an harmonious shapeliness upon a background of grim actuality, shot through at the same time, for all its sternness, with a radiant and transfiguring imagination. It is satire, poetry, realism, and high exuberant humour poured into and fused in the alembic of art.' (*Athenaeum*, June 8, 1912, pp. 664, 663). The great options the actors have to determine the mode of the play is also discussed by Thomas R. Whitaker in the Introduction to *Twentieth Century Interpretations of The Playboy*, pp. 13-14.

14. There is astringent irony in Synge's using *dream* to represent the Douls' futile ideals and *lie* to represent Christy's fecund one. The word *dream* occurs more than twenty times in *The Well of the Saints; lie* occurs less often in *Playboy*, but at crucial points.

15. The fullest discussion of this is James F. Kilroy's in 'The Playboy as Poet', in *PMLA*, LXXXIII (May 1968), 439-42. Also worthwhile is Patricia Meyer Spacks' 'The Making of the Playboy', in *Modern Drama*, IV (December 1961), 314-23.

16. I discuss language as the mediator between reality and imagination more fully in 'James Joyce and the Power of the Word', in *The Classic British Novel*, ed. Howard M. Harper, Jr and Charles Edge (Athens: Univ. of Georgia Press, 1972), pp. 183-201.

17. In *The Fall of Hyperion*, the shadowy Moneta challenges the poet:

> 'Art thou not of the dreamer tribe?
> The poet and the dreamer are distinct,
> Diverse, sheer opposite, antipodes.
> The one pours out a balm upon the World,
> The other vexes it.' (I, 198-202).

VI

A sense that fits him to perceive objects
unseen before: *Deirdre of the Sorrows*

Deirdre of the Sorrows is often seen as a new departure for Synge because in it he turns to Irish myth, a subject matter that, however common for his contemporaries, he had supposedly thus far disdained.[1] That Synge had not in fact ignored this material is shown by his several reviews and essays on early Irish literature (see *CW*, II, Part Four), and by his draft of the play 'Luasnad, Capa and Laine' (*CW*, III, 194-205). We know too that Synge read Irish myth at Trinity College and attended de Jubainville's lectures at the Sorbonne. And he showed an interest specifically in the Deirdre story as early as 1901 (Greene/Stephens, pp. 218-219). But the question remains, why Synge decided at this time to devote his energies to a major drama on a subject matter he had until now neglected.

The answer lies in the fruition in Synge's mind of realizations growing out of the themes we have been pursuing. As we shall see, what Synge disdained was not Irish myth, but his contemporaries' attitudes toward it. What encouraged him to turn to this subject matter was the realization that his fellow writers had fallen victims to a stereotyped view of the material, and the challenge of refusing to let that dictate his own attitude toward it. It is as if, in conscious application of the ideas he had been dramatizing, Synge set out to become aware of the other writers' implicit attitudes, and to make evading those a principle of his own approach. The result is a fresh, even unique, interpretation of the Deirdre story, one that might well shock anyone who expected another presentation tincted with Celtic twilight.

In terms of the themes we have been pursuing, then, *Deirdre* does represent a new departure for Synge. For the concern with challenging stereotypes enters this play in a more implicit and mature way than in earlier plays. One danger run by the dramatist who is strongly attracted to challenging received ideas is the temptation to place too much value on evoking and frustrating his audience's stereotypes, on puzzling or surprising his audience. The subject matter may then become a vehicle for the desired effect, and the plays become contrived, in the attempt to lead the audience through their paces and keep them on the edge of what they will tolerate. The result in some of Synge's earlier plays is an insistent, almost gratuitous toying with the audience's cherished ideas and mores.[2] In *Deirdre,* however, Synge keeps his eye on the careful and consistent development of his own conception of the story, without any finicky wish 'épater le bourgeois'. Here Synge's concern with received ideas occurs not in something he wishes to do to his audience, but in his own attitudes – in his intention to find a fresh perspective on material many others had already dramatized. This is not to say that Synge ignores audience psychology, but simply that he rises above any compulsion to surprise or confuse. The result is his achieving here a classic simplicity and tranquility of effect that the other plays lack.[3]

We know that Synge did not share his contemporaries' veneration of Irish myth or their hope of redeeming Ireland through its resurrection. In a carefully worded (even rewritten) letter responding to Stephen MacKenna's partial agreement with critics of *The Shadow of the Glen,* Synge said,

> I do not believe in the possibility of 'a purely fantastic, un-modern, ideal, breezy, springdayish, Cuchulainoid National Theatre'. . . . Of course it is possible to write drama that fills your description and yet is fitter for the stage than *The Shadowy Waters,* but no drama can grow out of anything other than the fundamental realities of modern life which are never fantastic, are neither modern nor unmodern and, as I see them, rarely spring-dayish, or breezy or Cuchulainoid.[4]

A similar attitude is implicit in Synge's poem 'The Passing of the Shee (after looking at one of A.E.'s pictures)':

> Adieu, sweet Angus, Maeve and Fand
> Ye plumed yet skinny Shee,
> That poets played with hand in hand
> To learn their ecstasy.

> We'll search in Red Dan Sally's ditch,
> And drink in Tubber Fair,
> Or poach with Red Dan Philly's bitch
> The badger and the hare. (*Coll. Works,* I, 38)

Since we know Synge did value early Irish literature, we can see that the object of satire here is not the characters, but the attitudes toward them of his contemporaries. As the contrasting stanzas of the poem imply, the writers have attenuated the mythic characters, depriving them of vitality. But Synge felt there might well be more human substance in these personages than his contemporaries had done justice to, and he became intrigued by the possibilities within the early stories.

That he regarded the Deirdre story as a challenge to his empathy and imagination is shown by a letter he wrote to John Quinn:

I don't know whether I told you that I am trying a three-act prose 'Deirdre', to change my hand. I am not sure yet whether I shall be able to make a satisfactory play out of it. These saga people, when one comes to deal with them, seem very remote; one does not know what they thought or what they are or where they went to sleep, so one is apt to fall into rhetoric. In any case, I find it an interesting experiment, full of new difficulties, and I shall be the better, I think, for the change. (*Coll. Works,* IV, xxvi).

This statement is important for our understanding Synge's objections to contemporary handlings of the myths, and his own aims. Synge wished to break through the insulation, the stereotypes, surrounding contemporary discussions of the myths, to see the characters not as mystical or heroic, but as men and women motivated by the same needs and fears, petty and great, that we are, and to see the stories and the characters from within. He wished to avoid the rhetoric that is the dress of stereotype, to empathize with the characters fully enough to know what they are, where they went to sleep. When Edward Stephens asked Synge about the danger that he would be accused of copying Yeats's or Russell's Deirdre plays, Synge replied, 'Oh no – there isn't any danger of that. People are entitled to use those old stories in any way they wish. My treatment of the story of Deirdre wouldn't be like either of theirs!' (Greene/Stephens, p. 277).

Here again we find a problem of perspective, of 'perceptual set', analogous to what we have seen before, for Synge's aim was to evade the attitudes the others had toward the myths, to abjure mysticism or heroism as the received modes for viewing the stories and to get closer to the humanity of the persons and events. If he could do this, if he could achieve a fresh perception of the material, uncolored by contemporary cliches, there would truly be no danger of his duplicating Yeats or A.E.[5]

A passage in the Greene/Stephens biography describes the challenge Synge faced:

> Instead of working directly from a folk tale he had heard or an incident of peasant life he had seen, he was attempting to breathe life into the 'rare and royal names wormy sheepskin yet retains', as he phrased it in his poem 'Queens', by visualizing them as the simple but passionate people he had known in the west of Ireland and in the hills of Wicklow. The problem was a linguistic one. (Greene/Stephens, p. 219).

But while it is true that he wished to breathe life into these characters, it is wrong to make the peasants his standard or to describe his problem as linguistic. His problem was conceptual and psychological, in that he had to be able to conceive of these people fully enough to attribute to them realistic motives for what they did. And his model was not the peasants, but the people surrounding him every day, especially his fiancée, Molly Allgood.[6]

Synge did succeed in meeting the challenge the material provided, and the result was a presentation of the Deirdre story that is far more psychologically complex than those offered by his contemporaries. One of Synge's strengths is his ability to present complex, multi-level psychology among his characters, and here his achievement appears the more distinctive because of the blandness of others' presentations. One result of this penchant for complex psychology is that many of Synge's plays contain crucial or climactic scenes in which a character does something apparently inconsistent or self-contradictory, something that expresses the surfacing of some subliminal, perhaps unconscious, motivation. We see this in Nora's leaving with the tramp, in Sarah's fury against the priest, in the violence and bitterness of Pegeen's attack on Christy. Here it appears in Deirdre's puzzling, wilful attempt to keep Naisi from aiding his brothers as they are attacked by Conchubor's forces.

For many critics the heart of the play is its presentation of the tragedy or pathos of this traditional story, its evocation of the themes of fate and the transiency of love and of life, and of the treachery men are driven to by strong emotions. For me, however, the heart of the play is Synge's conception of Deirdre as a strong-willed, selfish, and radically romantic young woman. If my view of the play is different, and darker, than most, it arises out of the necessity to make sense of some crucial psychological relationships in the play that go largely undiscussed, almost unnoticed, by others.

Synge's play does of course adhere to the lines of the traditional story, so that the prophecy is fulfilled, but nowhere does Synge evoke a sense of fate as an overriding power. The characters talk and act as if they have some influence over what happens. Lavarcham's charge to Deirdre, 'Are you choosing this night to destroy the world?' (*Coll. Works*, IV, 213) certainly has that implication. An apparent contradiction to this is Deirdre's occasional lament, especially early in act two when she says: '[*without hope*] There's little power in oaths to stop what's coming and little power in what I'd do, Lavarcham, to change the story of Conchubor and Naisi and the things old men foretold.' (*Coll. Works*, IV, 217). But the passage probably reflects Deirdre's boredom and loneliness more than a conviction of the inescapability of the prophecy, for her attitudes and actions contradict this later in the act when she first agrees to let Naisi make the choice about returning, and later herself chooses to return. Nowhere does Deirdre seem to take the prophecy fatalistically, i.e. in such a way as to believe that her acts have no power.

Synge's presentation focuses not so much on Deirdre's fate or on any all-compelling love for Naisi that she feels, but on her self-centred wish to be free of the old king. She tells Conchubor that she had rather stay where she is than be his queen in Emain, that she wants her freedom on the hills, that 'I'm too long taking my will, and it's that way I'll be living always.' (*Coll. Works*, IV, 193, 195). Her first reference to Naisi reflects not love, but a hope of finding someone who has the courage to oppose Conchubor (IV, 197), and her later appeal to Naisi to take her away expresses fear of going with Conchubor much more than love of Naisi: 'You must not go, Naisi, and leave me to the High King, a man is ageing in his Dun, with his crowds round him and his silver and gold. [*More quickly.*] I will not live to be shut up in Emain, and wouldn't we do well paying, Naisi, with silence, and a near death?' (IV, 211).

If the prophecy enters at all into the psychology, it appears as a romantic fascination on the part of Deirdre, who says to Naisi, 'It should be a sweet thing to have what is best and richest if it's for a short space only' (IV, 209), and then 'Won't I be in great dread to bring you to destruction, Naisi, and you so happy and young?' (IV, 211). When Lavarcham challenges Deirdre about the effects her selfish actions will have – 'Are you choosing this night to destroy the world?' – Deirdre replies (*'very deliberately'*) 'It's Conchubor has chosen this night calling me to Emain' (IV, 213), thus claiming to free herself from all responsibility for what happens.

In act two, set in Alban seven years later, Deirdre and Naisi have enjoyed seven years of love, but Deirdre is not content. She tells Lavarcham,

> It's lonesome this place having happiness like ours till I'm asking each day, will this day match yesterday, and will to-morrow take a good place beside the same day in the year that's gone, and wondering all times is it a game worth playing, living on until you're dried and old, and our joy is gone forever. (IV, 219).

While a certain amount of this attitude is inherent in human nature and is desirable, Deirdre has it in excess. Lavarcham presents a more sober perspective when she tells her,

> If it's that ails you, I tell you there's little hurt getting old, though young girls and poets do be storming at the shapes of age. [*Passionately.*] There's little hurt getting old, saving when you're looking back the way I'm looking this day, and seeing the young you have a love for breaking up their hearts with folly. (IV, 219).

Deirdre wants no such counsel, for it might dilute her romanticism, a romanticism that can never be satisfied by even the best of all possible experiences, because that experience cannot be sustained, and it becomes an unmatchable standard for whatever follows. The better today is, the worse tomorrow will be by comparison. This is extreme romanticism, of the sort drama-tized by Keats in his odes, and depicted by Flaubert in Emma Bovary.

Naisi shares Deirdre's feelings, though in less radical form, and he confides to Fergus, 'I'll not tell you a lie. There have been days a while past when I've been throwing a line for salmon, or watching for the run of hares, that I've had a dread upon me a day'd come I'd weary of her voice [*very slowly*] . . . and Deirdre'd see I'd wearied.' (IV, 227). But in Naisi this inevitable human fear is not allowed to develop into a life-corroding romanticism.

He decides, 'I'll not go, Fergus. I've had dreams of getting old and weary, and losing my delight in Deirdre, but my dreams were dreams only' (IV, 229), and he accepts the challenge of the future: 'But this talk's brought me ease, and I see we're as happy as the leaves on the young trees and we'll be so ever and always though we'd live the age of the eagle and the salmon and the crow of Britain.' (IV, 229).

But Deirdre has heard Naisi's talk with Fergus, and his admission of fear about the future does what Owen's arguments could not – determines her return to Ireland. Naisi has faced and quelled the inescapable lover's fears of the decline of love – has vowed to make the future as full as the past and present; Lavarcham has told her that growing old is not terrible, and that its greatest hurt is seeing the young people one loves hurting themselves. But when Deirdre overhears Naisi's admission of fear, her resolve to stay in Alban, or at least to let Naisi make the decision, collapses. She tells Naisi:

> There's no place to stay always. . . . It's a long time we've had, pressing the lips together, going up and down, resting in our arms, Naisi, waking with the smell of June in the tops of the grasses, and listening to the birds in the branches that are highest. . . . It's a long time we've had, but the end has come surely. (IV, 231).

Naisi wavers and, contrary to the resolve he expressed to Fergus, gives in: 'You're right maybe. . . . It should be a poor thing to see great lovers and they sleepy and old' (IV, 233), and he agrees with Deirdre that 'we'll go surely, in place of keeping a watch on a love had no match and it wasting away'. (IV, 233).

This is the thematic and psychological crisis of the play; from here it moves with quickening pace toward the necessary conclusion – old Conchubor's treachery, and the deaths of Naisi and Deirdre. Both Deirdre and Naisi know what their choice involves; they know that they are choosing to let death eclipse their great love rather than see it wane. But in the third act of the play, something unforeseen, something puzzling and almost perverse happens, and we must look closely at it if we are to appreciate the psychological intricacy of the drama.

Both Naisi and Deirdre know that they have made a bargain for death, and they approach death with acceptance, almost recklessly. But as the battle outside mounts and Naisi prepares to join his brothers in their last fight, Deirdre makes an intolerable claim on her husband. She beseeches him not to go to them, but to stay with her. Then follows this crucial passage:

AINNLE [*behind*]. Naisi . . . Naisi. . . . Come to us, we are betrayed and broken.

NAISI. It's Ainnle crying out in a battle!

CONCHUBOR. I was near won this night, but death's between us now.

[*He goes out.*]

DEIRDRE [*clinging to* NAISI]. There is no battle. . . . Do not leave me, Naisi.

NAISI. I must go to them.

DEIRDRE [*beseechingly*]. Do not leave me, Naisi. Let us creep up in the darkness behind the grave. . . . If there's a battle, maybe the strange fighters will be destroyed, when Ainnle and Ardan are against them.

[*Cries are heard.*]

NAISI [*wildly*]. I hear Ardan crying out. Do not hold me from my brothers.

DEIRDRE [*broken after the strain*]. Do not leave me, Naisi. Do not leave me broken and alone.

NAISI. I cannot leave my brothers when it is I who have defied the king.

DEIRDRE. I will go with you.

NAISI. You cannot come. . . . Do not hold me from the fight.

[*He throws her aside almost roughly.*]

DEIRDRE [*with restraint*]. Go to your brothers. . . . For seven years you have been kindly, but the hardness of death has come between us.

NAISI [*looking at her aghast*]. And you'll have me meet death with a hard word from your lips in my ear?

DEIRDRE. We've had a dream, but this night has waked us surely. In a little while we've lived too long, Naisi, and isn't it a poor thing we should miss the safety of the grave, and we trampling its edge?

AINNLE [*behind*]. Naisi, Naisi, we are attacked and ruined.

DEIRDRE. Let you go where they are calling! [*She looks at him for an instant coldly.*] Have you no shame loitering and talking and a cruel death facing Ainnle and Ardan in the woods?

NAISI [*frantic*]. They'll not get a death that's cruel and they with men alone. It's women that have loved are cruel only, and if I went on living from this day I'd be putting a curse on the lot of them I'd meet walking in the east or west, putting a curse on the sun that gave them beauty, and on the madder and the stone-crop put red upon their cloaks.

DEIRDRE [*bitterly*]. I'm well pleased there's no one this place to make a story that Naisi was a laughing-stock the night he died.

NAISI. There'd not be many'd make a story, for that mockery is in your eyes this night will spot the face of Emain with a plague of pitted graves. [*He draws out his sword, throws down belt and cloak, and goes out.*] (*Coll. Works*, IV, 255, 257).

I have quoted this passage at length because it is crucial to my view of the play and it deserves scrutiny. We must make out what is going on here. Has Deirdre really become so frightened that she cannot let Naisi do what he must? And why, when she tells him to go, does she do it so severely? Certainly Naisi does not understand what is happening; he is bewildered, hurt, 'aghast'. And what are we to make of Deirdre's cruelty to Naisi, toying with him and accusing him of loitering shamelessly while his brothers die? Naisi, frantic, says, 'They'll not get a death that's cruel and they with men alone. It's women that have loved are cruel only.'

This act of Deirdre's is the epitome of her hypertrophied romanticism, for in her toying with Naisi, there is a perverse wish to bring to the most poignant pitch possible the end of their lives together. What could be more dramatic, more romantic, than to have loved one another faithfully to the very edge of the grave, and then to lose the sanctity of that love! How heartrending to think of Naisi going to his death not in the confidence of love, but with bitterness and regret and mockery tainting it. Deirdre's purpose here, which preempts whatever warmth or solace she is prompted to show to Naisi, is to achieve for their story a truly dramatic end, one that will indeed be told forever. There is a terrifying satisfaction in her claim to Conchubor, 'It was my words without pity gave Naisi a death will have no match until the ends of life and time.' (IV, 257).[7]

In presenting his rendering of the Deirdre legend, Synge did not set out to twist the plot so as to puzzle his audience. He sought instead to delve into the characters and psychology of the story deeply enough to see the relationships as specific and personal rather than general and mythic. He wished to envision the characters in terms of his own understanding of psychology, as he saw it in the people around him, and to see what labyrinthine windings of motive the story might encourage or at least permit. If my reading of Deirdre's character is correct, Synge succeeded in doing this, for he broke through the stereotyped attitudes toward the myth to produce a distinctive portrait of Deirdre and a complex interpretation of her relationship with Naisi. In doing so, he transmuted what had once been a source of trauma for him into a liberating principle. Rather than falling victim of the received attitudes toward the mythic material, Synge sought out those attitudes and used his awareness of them as an aid to discovering his own distinctive interpretation.

NOTES TO CHAPTER VI

1. For a survey of critical comments on the play, see pp. 350-354 of my 'J. M. Synge' in *Anglo-Irish Literature: A Review of Research* (New York, 1976).
2. We have already noted in footnote 4 to Chapter IV, some evidence of Synge's wishing to push his audiences' sensibilities to the breaking point. Furthermore, the drafts of *The Tinker's Wedding* contain expressions that no contemporary audience could have accepted : Sarah was to have said that she had 'as good a right to a decent marriage as any speckled female bastard does be sleeping in the black hovels' (*Coll. Works*, IV, 34), and Mary was to have said to the struggling priest, 'Let you not be walloping the earth for fatness is a nasty thing, your reverence, and the sweat out of you would stink the nation with your struggling now' (*Coll. Works*, IV, 46), and in another place, Synge changed *shift* to *clothes* in galley proof. (*Coll. Works*, IV, 32). There is then, some basis for the charge that Francis Sheehy-Skeffington made in a letter sympathetic to Synge and the *Playboy*. Of that play's language he said, 'I am not squeamish, and have no puritanical objection to strong language on the stage, provided it can be made to subserve an artistic purpose. But here it appeared to be gratuitously dragged in, as if the author had set himself to find out exactly how much his audience would stand. If that were his object, he achieved it.' (Quoted in James Kilroy, *The Playboy Riots*, p. 21.)
3. Synge's only other play in which I feel a similar effect is *Riders to the Sea*. In *Riders* and in *Deirdre*, Synge's wish to do justice to his subject matter counterbalances the concern for audience manipulation we find in the other plays. The debate that has gathered around the generic category and world view of *Riders to the Sea* results not from Synge's having set out intentionally to breach generic lines, but simply from his truthfully depicting a situation the Western mind has no ready responses to.
4. The letter is printed in Greene/Stephens, pp. 156-158. The phrase Synge quotes was in MacKenna's letter to Synge.

5. Synge's wish to make his play more realistic than those of Yeats and A.E. has been discussed by several critics. See, for example, Donna Gerstenberger, *John Millington Synge*, pp. 96 ff.

6. Edward M. Stephens, Synge's nephew, stresses how much Synge drew on personal experiences in writing the play in 'Synge's Last Play'. (*Contemporary Review*, CLXXXVI, Nov. 1954, pp. 288-93). He says that Synge's 'writings were always inspired by his personal experience' (p. 288), and traces many of Synge's interests in *Deirdre* to his developing relationship with Molly. He contends, for example, that Synge's joyful experiences with Molly in Glen Cree in July 1907, 'inspired the dramatization of Naisi in the woods with Deirdre' (p. 291).

7. I said earlier that the psychology here owes something to Synge's relationship with Molly. I do not imply that Deirdre was simply a depiction of her – I know too little of her personality to make that ungenerous suggestion. From Synge's letters to Molly, we know that he did see her as self-centred, fickle, inconsiderate, immature, but this is a far cry from the perverse romanticism of Deirdre. Synge need not have had a specific model for his depiction; he knew many persons and he had considerable imagination. And he may even have had some romantic quirks himself, for his letters occasionally suggest that he enjoyed looking forward to seeing Molly, and complaining about all the things that kept them apart, almost as much as he enjoyed being with her.

Conclusion

This book has called into question the ideas generally held by critics of Synge that the religious milieu he was reared in had little influence on him, that his familial relationships meant little to him, and that he cared little for matters of 'belief' generally. The view presented here is that Synge was always more concerned about beliefs than he appeared to be, and that the theme of the relationship between 'beliefs' and 'reality' is basic to his work.

Contrary to general opinion, Synge was quite sensitive to the religious milieu of his family and was deeply concerned that he could not accept their religious doctrines. He did not in fact reject their religious concerns, but rather he transformed them into ideas about personality and art. His inability to dissemble or to pretend to beliefs he did not have, and his sense of stewardship – of the artist as having an obligation to use his gifts – are two examples of his translating his family's religious values into his own terms. And rather than being indifferent to matters of belief, he seems to have been supersensitive to them, so much so that he could not simply debate them as theories. His frequently noted taciturnity more likely implies an inability to banter about matters of belief than an indifference to them. Further, his family's emphasis on doctrine and on the necessity of intellectual accord militated against Synge's natural sensitivity to affective tone and his inclination to value emotive unities over intellectual ones. In short, the young Synge was in several ways victimized by received attitudes and modes of thought.

Seen in this context, Synge's experiences on the Aran Islands take on a deeper, clearer significance. On these islands Synge lived in a milieu governed by received ideas qualitatively different from those he had been reared in. This had two main effects: first, some of the received ideas of this archiac culture seemed to him more appealing, more conducive to an organic, wholistic, view of life, than had his family's ideas. These provided him with a paradigm of how man and nature should relate, and led to a clarification of his own ideas about art. Second, the great differ-

ences between the assumptions of this culture and his own precipitated an awareness of how variable and how arbitrary the
received notions of any culture may be, and of how large a role
received ideas play in our own apprehension of reality and the
tonality of our experience. As he digested these realizations
(mainly through writing *The Aran Islands*), the variety and pervasiveness of such implicit perspectives became clearer to him,
and generated themes and devices that became the staples of his
drama.

Each of Synge's first three plays involves some specific reflection of what he realized through his experiences on the islands. In
The Shadow of the Glen Synge intentionally varies the plot of a
story he heard on the islands, so as to draw his audience into a
familiar stereotype. But having done this, he then shatters the
stereotype and throws his audience into the confusion that results
when our expectations, our perceptual sets, are frustrated. The
result is to put his audience through a perceptual and intellectual
shock analogous to what Synge himself had undergone upon reading Darwin or upon imbibing the milieu of the islands.

In *Riders to the Sea,* Synge tries to present as veridically as
possible the quality of life he felt on the islands. His aim was to
be faithful to the tone and mood, to the affective realities, of that
world. But as the reaction to the play shows, most critics have
been unable to respond to that world without attempting to
pigeonhole the play in terms of genre or of world view. The result
is a body of critical discussion largely irrelevant to the play, and
another illustration of the authority of received categories of
thought.

The Tinker's Wedding focuses directly upon 'cultural relativism' by depicting a contrast between the world view of the
tinkers and that of the priest. The theme we are tracing enters
the play primarily in the invasion of young Mary Byrne's world
by an abstraction from the other society; through Mary's superficial aspiration to marriage, Synge explores the folly and frustration of trying to fit one's experience into a social or intellectual
frame unnatural to it. The marriage ritual is as procrustean to her
experience as the marriage ring is to her finger.

In *The Well of the Saints* and *The Playboy of the Western
World,* Synge moves into a new phase of his response to his
experiences on the islands, one characterized by pursuing certain
philosophical issues raised by these themes, especially the problem of the relationship between our ideas, or dreams, or hopes,
and 'reality'. In *The Well of the Saints,* he rather disturbingly

suggests through the Douls that there need be only a minimal connection between the two – that we can perhaps live with a 'dream' that runs so counter to reality that it is in fact a lie. Critics have responded variously to the confrontation between truth and reality in the play. Some say it expresses a nihilism Synge himself espoused; others find it inconsistent with Synge's own world-view; others simply extol it as presenting a sort of existential freedom. My own response is that the relation between dream and reality in the play is nihilistic, but that this is a necessary, almost predictable, part of Synge's exploration of some of the darker aspects of his theme, and that we need not see it as more than exploration – need not take it as an indication of what Synge himself believes.

The idea that *The Well of the Saints* is exploratory rather than definitive is supported by the fact that *Playboy* offers a more subtle and satisfactory presentation of this same theme. In *Playboy,* in contrast to the earlier play, abstraction and reality are not presented as static and mutually exclusive, but as kinetic and interpenetrating. In a presentation that suggests his deeper insight into the power of language as mediator between imagination and reality, Synge shows us through Christy's being made a man 'by the power of a lie', that the imagination and reality are complementary. Christy's 'lie', in contrast to that of the Douls, does not run counter to reality, but runs parallel to it, and influences it. In coming to this more complex and satisfying grasp of the philosophical issues within this theme, Synge completed an important phase of his concern with it.

In *Deirdre of the Sorrows,* Synge's interest in the power of stereotypes emerges in a different way. Here it appears not as the need *épater le bourgeois,* or to foil abstraction and reality, but as a conscious wish on Synge's part to break through the stereotyped way that the myth had been responded to by earlier writers. Realizing that even Yeats and A.E. had permitted themselves to be drawn into regarding the Deirdre story through the rose-tinted glass of beautiful myth, Synge set himself the challenge of regarding the personages as real people, with mixed but tangible motives. The distinctiveness of his version derives mainly from his having succeeded in doing this, and shows how completely he had transformed his concern with the power of the stereotype from a realization to be articulated or a philosophical problem to be solved, into a tool to facilitate finding his own viewpoint.

Bibliography

Manuscript Material

Notebooks, diaries, letters, drafts, etc. in the Manuscript Collection of Trinity College, Dublin.

Edward M. Stephens' Typescript biography of his uncle, J. M. Synge.

Printed Material

Allport, Floyd H. *Theories of Perception and the Concept of Structure.* New York: John Wiley & Sons, 1955. xxii, 709 pp.

[Anonymous]. 'The Irish Players'. *Athenaeum,* June 8, 1912, pp. 663-64.

Ayling, Ronald. 'Synge's First Love: Some South African Aspects'. *Modern Drama,* VI (February 1964), 450-60.

Bessai, Diane E. 'Little Hound in Mayo: Synge's *Playboy* and the Comic Tradition in Irish Literature'. *Dalhousie Review,* XLVIII (Autumn 1968), 372-83.

Binchy, D. A. 'The Linguistic and Historical Value of the Irish Law Tracts'. *Proceedings of the British Academy,* XXIX (1943), 195-227.

Birmingham, George A. 'The Literary Movement in Ireland'. *Fortnightly Review,* LXXXII (December 2, 1907), 947-57.

Bourgeois, Maurice. *John Millington Synge and the Irish Theatre.* New York and London: Benjamin Blom, 1968. xvi, 338 pp. A reprint of the book first published in 1913 by Constable.

Brehm, Jack W., and Arthur R. Cohen. *Explorations in Cognitive Dissonance.* New York: John Wiley & Sons, 1962. xvi, 334 pp.

Bushrui, S. B., ed. *Sunshine and the Moon's Delight: A Centenary Tribute to John Millington Synge 1871-1909.* Gerrards Cross and Beirut: Colin Smythe Ltd., and the American University of Beirut, 1972. 356 pp.

Calder-Marshall, Arthur. *The Innocent Eye: The Life of Robert J. Flaherty.* New York: Harcourt, Brace & World, Inc., 1966. 306 pp. Illustrations.

Clark, David R., ed. *John Millington Synge: Riders to the Sea*. Columbus, Ohio: Charles E. Merrill Publishing Co., 1970. vi, 137 pp. In the Merrill Literary Casebook Series.

—————————. 'Synge's "Perpetual 'Last Day' "': Remarks on *Riders to the Sea'*. S. B. Bushrui, ed., *Sunshine and the Moon's Delight* (1972), pp. 41-51.

Colum, Padraic. *The Road Round Ireland*. New York: Macmillan, 1926. 492 pp.

Combs, William W. 'J. M. Synge's *Riders to the Sea:* A Reading and Some Generalizations'. *Papers of the Michigan Academy of Science, Arts, and Letters,* L (1965), 599-607.

Corkery, Daniel. *Synge and Anglo-Irish Literature*. Dublin and Cork: Cork University Press, 1931. 247 pp.

Dillon, Myles. 'The Archaism of Irish Tradition'. *Proceedings of the British Academy*, XXXIII (1947), 245-64.

————————— and Nora Chadwick. *The Celtic Realms*. London: Weidenfeld and Nicholson, 1967. xii, 355 pp. plates, maps.

Donoghue, Denis. 'Synge: "Riders to the Sea": A Study'. *University Review,* I (Summer 1955), 52-58. Reprinted in David R. Clark's casebook on *Riders to the Sea*.

Dorson, Richard M. 'Foreword' to Sean O'Sullivan, ed. *Folktales of Ireland,* pp. v-xxxii.

Ellis-Fermor, Una. *The Irish Dramatic Movement*. London: Methuen & Co., Ltd., 1967. xiv, 241 pp. (A University Paperback reprint of the second edition [1954] of this book, which first appeared in 1939.)

Ellmann, Richard. *James Joyce*. New York: Oxford University Press, 1959. 842 pp.

Estill, Adelaide Duncan. *The Sources of Synge*. Philadelphia: [University of Pennsylvania?], 1939. 51 pp.

Evans, E. Estyn. *Irish Folk Ways*. London: Routledge and Kegan Paul, 1957. xvi, 324 pp.

Fausset, Hugh l'A. 'Synge and Tragedy'. *Fortnightly Review*, CXV (February 1, 1924), 258-73.

Festinger, Leon. *Conflict, Decision, and Dissonance*. Stanford, Calif.: Stanford University Press, 1964. xii, 163 pp.

—————————. *A Theory of Cognitive Dissonance*. Stanford, Calif.: Stanford University Press, 1962. xii, 291 pp. (First published by Row, Peterson and Company in 1957.)

Flower, Robin. *The Western Island or The Great Blasket*. New York: Oxford University Press, 1945. 138 pp.

Gailey, R. A. 'Aspects of Change in a Rural Community'. *Ulster Folklife,* V (1959), 27-34.

Galsworthy, John. *The Inn of Tranquillity: Studies and Essays.* London: William Heinemann, 1912. 278 pp.

Gerstenberger, Donna. *John Millington Synge.* New York: Twayne Publishers Inc., 1964. 157 pp. Twayne's English Authors Series, No. 12.

Greene, David H., and Edward M. Stephens. *J. M. Synge 1871-1909.* New York: The Macmillan Co., 1959. xiv, 321 pp. The Collier paperback reprint of this work (1961) is marred by many typographical errors.

Greene, David H. 'The Shadow of the Glen and the Widow of Ephesus'. *PMLA,* LXII (March 1947), 233-38.

Gregory, Lady Augusta. *Our Irish Theatre.* New York: Capricorn Books, 1965. A paperback edition of the book first published by G. P. Putnam in 1913.

——————. *Visions and Beliefs in the West of Ireland Collected and Arranged by Lady Gregory: With Two Essays and Notes by W. B. Yeats.* Gerrards Cross: Colin Smythe, 1970. 365 pp. Vol. I of the Coole edition of Lady Gregory's Works. This book was first published in 1920, by G. P. Putnam's Sons.

Grene, Nicholas. *Synge: A Critical Study of the Plays.* Totowa, New Jersey: Rowman and Littlefield, 1975. 202 pp.

Harmon, Maurice, ed. *J. M. Synge Centenary Papers 1971.* Dublin: The Dolmen Press, 1972. xvi, 202 pp.

Hart, William. 'Synge's Ideas on Life and Art: Design and Theory in *The Playboy of the Western World*'. *Yeats Studies,* No. 2 (1972), 35-51.

Henn, T. R., ed. *The Plays and Poems of J. M. Synge.* London: Methuen and Co., Ltd., 1968. (University Paperback Drama Book edition; the original was published in 1963.)

Holloway, Joseph. *Joseph Holloway's Abbey Theatre: A Selection from his Unpublished Journal Impressions of a Dublin Playgoer,* ed. Robert Hogan and Michael O'Neill. Carbondale and Edwardsville, Ill.: Southern Illinois University Press, 1967. xxiv, 296 pp.

Howe, P. P. *J. M. Synge: A Critical Study.* London: Martin Secker, 1912. 216 pp.

Hyde, Douglas. *A Literary History of Ireland.* London: T. Fisher Unwin, 1899. 654 pp. Reprinted by Barnes and Noble, 1967.

Jackson, Kenneth Hurlstone. *The Oldest Irish Tradition: A Window on the Iron Age.* Cambridge: Cambridge University Press, 1964. 56 pp.

Johnston, Denis. *John Millington Synge.* New York and London:

Columbia University Press, 1965. 48 pp. Columbia Essays on Modern Writers, No. 12.

Kilroy, James F. 'The Playboy as Poet'. *PMLA*, LXXXIII (May 1968), 439-42.

—————. *The 'Playboy' Riots*. Dublin: The Dolmen Press, 1971. 101 pp. The Irish Theatre series, No. 4.

Kelsall, Malcolm. 'Synge in Aran', *Irish University Review*, V, 2 (Autumn 1975), 254-270.

Keohler, Thomas. 'The Irish National Theatre'. *Dana*, No. 11 (March 1905), 351-52.

Lawrence, D. H. 'Apropos of *Lady Chatterley's Lover*', preface to *Lady Chatterley's Lover*. London: William Heinemann Ltd., 1961. pp. 9-43.

—————. 'Art and Morality'. *Phoenix: The Posthumous Papers of D. H. Lawrence*. London: William Heinemann Ltd., 1936, pp. 521-26.

Levitt, Paul. *J. M. Synge: A Bibliography of Published Criticism*. New York: Barnes and Noble, 1974. 224 pp.

Lynch, Arthur. 'Synge'. *The Irish Statesman*, October 20, 1928, p. 131. (A letter to the editor.)

Macalister, R. A. S. *The Archaeology of Ireland*. Revised edition. London: Methuen and Co., Ltd., 1949. xx, 386 pp. plates, illustrations.

MacKenna, Stephen. *Journal and Letters of Stephen MacKenna*, ed. by E. R. Dodds. London: Constable and Co., Ltd., 1936. xvii, 330 pp. Dodds' Memoir is pp. 1-89. A Preface by Padraic Colum is on pp. xi-xvii.

MacMahon, Seán. '"Leave Troubling the Lord God": A Note on Synge and Religion'. *Éire-Ireland*, XI (Spring 1976), 132-141.

Masefield, John. *John M. Synge: A Few Personal Recollections with Biographical Notes by John Masefield*. New York: The Macmillan Co., 1915. 35 pp.

Mason, Thomas H. *The Islands of Ireland: Their Scenery, People, Life, and Antiquities*. 3rd ed. London: B. T. Batsford Ltd., 1950. viii, 135 pp. The first ed. was published in 1936.

[Matheson, Cherrie] C.H.H. 'John Synge as I Knew Him'. *The Irish Statesman*, July 5, 1924, pp. 532, 534. (Prefaced by a note by Yeats, 'A Memory of Synge', pp. 530, 532.)

Mercier, Vivian. *The Irish Comic Tradition*. Oxford: Clarendon Press, 1962. xx, 258 pp.

Meyer, Kuno, and Alfred Nutt. *The Voyage of Bran Son of Febal . . . With an Essay Upon the Irish Vision of the Happy*

Otherworld and the Celtic Doctrine of Rebirth. 2 vols. London: David Nutt, 1895, 1897.

Mikhail, E. H. *J. M. Synge: A Bibliography of Criticism.* Totowa, New Jersey: Rowman and Littlefield, 1975. 214 pp.

Mould, Daphne D. C. Pochin. *The Aran Islands.* Newton Abbot: David and Charles, Ltd., 1972. 171 pp.

Nic Shiubhlaigh, Maire. *The Splendid Years.* Dublin: James Duffy and Co., Ltd., 1955. xx. 207 pp. Foreword by Padraic Colum.

Nutt, Alfred. *The Celtic Doctrine of Rebirth*—see Meyer, Kuno, and Alfred Nutt.

O'Connor, Frank. 'Synge'. *The Irish Theatre,* ed. Lennox Robinson. London: Macmillan and Co., Ltd., 1939. xiv, 229 pp.

Ó Cuív, Brian, ed. *A View of the Irish Language.* Dublin: Stationery Office, 1969. x, 156 pp., plus 43 illustrations.

Ó Danachair, Caoimhín. 'The Gaeltacht'. Brian Ó Cuív, ed., *A View of the Irish Language,* pp. 112-21.

O'Driscoll, Robert. 'Yeats's Conception of Synge'. S. B. Bushrui, ed., *Sunshine and the Moon's Delight* (1972), pp. 159-71.

Ó Síocháin, P. A. *Aran: Islands of Legend.* 3rd ed. Dublin: Foilsiúcháin Éireann, 1967. viii, 200 pp. The first edition was published in 1962.

Ó Súilleabháin, Seán. 'Irish Oral Tradition'. Brian Ó Cuív, ed. *A View of the Irish Language,* pp. 47-56.

—————. *Irish Wake Amusements.* Cork: The Mercier Press, 1967. 188 pp. Translated by the author from the original Irish edition of 1961.

—————, ed. *Folktales of Ireland.* Chicago: University of Chicago Press, 1966. xliv, 321 pp.

Pittock, Malcolm. *'Riders to the Sea'. English Studies,* XLIX (October 1968), 445-49.

Price, Alan. *Synge and Anglo-Irish Drama.* London: Methuen and Co. Ltd., 1961. xii, 236 pp.

Rajan, Balachandra. 'Yeats, Synge and the Tragic Understanding'. *Yeats Studies,* No. 2 (1972), 66-79.

Rodgers, W. R. *Irish Literary Portraits.* London: British Broadcasting Corp., 1972. xx, 236 pp. 'J. M. Synge', pp. 94-115.

Saddlemyer, Ann, 'Art, Nature, and "The Prepared Personality": A Reading of *The Aran Islands* and Related Writings'. S. B. Bushrui, ed., *Sunshine and the Moon's Delight* (1972), pp. 107-20.

—————. '"A Share in the Dignity of the World": J. M. Synge's Aesthetic Theory.' Robin Skelton and Ann Saddlemyer, eds., *The World of W. B. Yeats,* rev. ed. Seattle: The

University of Washington Press, 1967. Essay is on pp. 207-19.

—————. 'Synge and Some Companions with a Note Concerning a Walk through Connemara with Jack Yeats'. *Yeats Studies,* No. 2 (1972), 18-34.

—————. 'Synge and the Doors of Perception', Andrew Carpenter, ed., *Place, Personality and the Irish Writer.* New York: Barnes and Noble, 1977. The essay is on pp. 97-120.

Skelton, Robin. *J. M. Synge and His World.* New York: The Viking Press, 1971. 144 pp. illustrations.

—————. *The Writings of J. M. Synge.* Indianapolis; New York: The Bobbs-Merrill Co., Inc., 1971. 190 pp.

Spacks, Patricia Meyer. 'The Making of the Playboy'. *Modern Drama,* IV (December 1961), 314-23.

Stephens, Edward. *My Uncle John: Edward Stephens's Life of J. M. Synge,* ed. Andrew Carpenter. London: Oxford University Press, 1974. xviii, 222 pp.

—————. 'Synge's Last Play'. *Contemporary Review,* CLXXXVI (November 1954), 288-93.

Suss, Irving D. 'The "Playboy" Riots'. *Irish Writing,* No. 18 (March 1952), 39-42.

Synge, John Millington. *Collected Works,* ed. Robin Skelton, Alan Price, and Ann Saddlemyer. London: Oxford University Press, 1962-1968. Volume I (1962) is edited by Robin Skelton (who is also the General Editor), and contains Synge's Poems, Translations, and some Poetic Drama. Vol. II (1966) is edited by Alan Price and contains Synge's Prose: Autobiographical Sketches; *The Aran Islands;* In Wicklow, West Kerry and Connemara; and various Reviews and Essays or Notes about Literature. Vol. III (1968) is edited by Ann Saddlemyer and contains *Riders to the Sea; The Shadow of the Glen; The Well of the Saints; When the Moon Has Set;* Fifteen Scenarios, Dialogues, and Fragments from Unpublished Material; and draft material and considerable editorial apparatus on the above. Vol. IV (1968) is edited by Ann Saddlemyer and contains *The Tinker's Wedding; The Playboy of the Western World; Deirdre of the Sorrows;* and considerable draft material and editorial apparatus on them.

—————. *John Millington Synge: Some Unpublished Letters and Documents of J. M. Synge. . . .* Montreal: The Redpath Press, 1959. 33 pp.

—————. 'Letters of John Millington Synge From Materials Supplied by Max Meyerfeld'. *The Yale Review,* XIII (July 1924), 690-709.

————————. *Letters to Molly: John Millington Synge to Maire O'Neill 1906-1909*, ed. Ann Saddlemyer. Cambridge, Mass.: The Belknap Press of Harvard Univerity Press, 1971. xxxiv, 330 pp.

The Synge Manuscripts in the Library of Trinity College, Dublin: A Catalogue Prepared on the Occasion of the Synge Centenary Exhibition 1971. Dublin: The Dolmen Press, 1971. 55 pp. Printed for the Library of Trinity College, Dublin.

Thornton, Weldon. 'James Joyce and the Power of the Word'. *The Classic British Novel*, ed. Howard M. Harper Jr and Charles Edge. Athens: University of Georgia Press, 1972. Pp. 183-201.

————————. 'J. M. Synge'. Richard J. Finneran, ed. *Anglo-Irish Literature: A Review of Research*. New York: The Modern Language Association, 1976, pp. 315-365.

Van Laan, Thomas F. 'Form as Agent in Synge's *Riders to the Sea*'. *Drama Survey, III* (Winter 1964), 352-66. Reprinted in David R. Clark's casebook on *Riders to the Sea*.

Whitaker, Thomas R. 'Introduction: On Playing with The Playboy'. *Twentieth Century Interpretations of The Playboy of the Western World*. Englewood Cliffs, New Jersey: 1969. pp. 1-20.

————————, ed. *Twentieth Century Interpretations of The Playboy of the Western World*. Englewood Cliffs, New Jersey: Prentice-Hall, Inc., 1969. 122 pp.

Whitehead, Alfred North. *Science and the Modern World*. New York: The Free Press, 1967: The book was first published in 1925.

Williams, Raymond. *Drama from Ibsen to Eliot*. London: Chatto and Windus, 1952. 283 pp. A revised edition appeared as *Drama from Ibsen to Brecht* (New York: Oxford Univ. Press, 1969).

Yeats, William Butler. *The Autobiography of William Butler Yeats*. New York: Collier Books, 1965. 404 pp. The Collier paperbook edition.

————————. *A Vision*. New York: Macmillan, 1961, 305 pp. The Macmillan paperback edition.

————————. *Essays and Introductions*. New York: Collier Books, 1968. xii, 530 pp.

Index

Stokes, William
  *The Life and Labours in Art
    and Archaeology of George
    Petrie,* 35
Suss, Irving D., 142
Swedenborg, Emanuel
  Heaven and Hell, 28
Synge, Alec, 38
Synge, Annnie, 17
Synge, Edward, 17, 22
Synge, John Millington
  his aesthetic, 19, 24-25, 28-29,
    35-36
  and the Aran Islands, 11-12, 13,
    14, 27, 41, 43-45, 50, 63,
    75 ff, 97-98, 106-107,
    155-156
  and his family 11, 12, 13-14,
    15, 6 ff, 62, 155
  and music, 35-36, 48
  and politics, 30-34
  and rationalism, 12, 16, 27, 41
  and religion, 11, 12, 13, 16 ff,
    27 ff, 40-41, 47
  and theoretical questions, 26 ff
  The Aran Islands, 14, 59, 63,
    74 ff, 108, 109, 156
  'Autobiography,' 17-18, 19, 27,
    32, 33, 41-42
  Deirdre of the Sorrows, 14, 99,
    108, 113, 128, 144-154, 157
  'A Dream on Inishmaan', 87-88
  'Glencullen,' 72
  'Luasnad, Capa and Laine,' 144
  Manchester Guardian articles,
    30
  Notebooks, 12, 19-20, 24, 25,
    29, 58
  'The Passing of the Shee,' 145
  'A Play of '98,' 100, 123
  Playboy of the Western World,
    97, 98, 100, 104, 108, 127-128,
    133, 134-141, 147, 156-157
Synge, John Millington
  Riders to the Sea, 74, 108-118,
    129, 133, 134, 154, 156
  Shadow of the Glen, 74, 97,

    99-107, 108, 110, 114, 118,
    128, 134, 145, 147, 156
  Tinker's Wedding, 74, 97, 100,
    118-123, 134, 147, 153, 156
  'La Vielle Litterature
    Irlandaise,' 58
  Well of the Saints, 99, 108,
    127-133, 134, 139-141,
    156-157
  When the Moon Has Set, 29,
    98
Synge, Mrs Kathleen, 17, 21, 22 ff,
  31, 32, 34, 37, 38, 46-47, 94
Synge, Mary, 36, 38
Synge, Robert, 17, 22, 31, 37,
  48, 94
Synge, Samuel, 17, 22, 48

Táin Bó Cúailgne, 56-57
Tauler, Rev John
  *The History and Life of the
    Reverend John Tauler,* 28-29
Tennyson, Alfred, 1st Baron, 33
Thomas à Kempis
  The Imitation of Christ, 28
Thornton, Weldon, 143
Traill, Anthony, 21
Trench, Archbishop Richard
  Chenevix, 73
  English Past and Present, 73
Trinity College, Dublin, 12, 18,
  19, 21, 34-36, 48, 144

Van Laan, Thomas F., 113
Von Eiken, Claire, 39
Von Eiken, Emma, 39
Von Eiken, Valeska, 37, 39-40

Wake, Irish, 65-69
Wakeman, William, F.
  Handbook of Irish Antiquities,
    35
Wallace, A. R.,
  *Miracles and Modern
    Spiritualism,* 28